WELL CONNECTED

Power Your Own Soul

by Plugging into Others

DIANNA BOOHER

WORD PUBLISHING

NASHVILLE

A Thomas Nelson Company

Well Connected
by Dianna Booher

Copyright © 2000 Dianna Booher
Published by Word Publishing, a division of Thomas Nelson, Inc.
P.O. Box 141000, Nashville, TN 37214.

Unless otherwise indicated, Scripture quotations used in this book are from the
Holy Bible, New International Version (NIV). Copyright © 1973, 1978, 1984,
International Bible Society. Used by permission of Zondervan Bible Publishers.

Published in association with the literary agency of Alive Communications, Inc.,
1465 Kelly Johnson Blvd., Suite 320, Colorado Springs, CO 80920.

Library of Congress Cataloging-in-Publication Data

Booher, Dianna
    Well connected: power your own soul by plugging into others / by Dianna
Booher.
     p. cm.
    Includes bibliographical references.
    ISBN 0-8499-3736-1
    1. Christian women—Religious life. 2. Interpersonal relations—Religious
aspects—Christianity. I. Title.

BV4527.W645 2000
248.4—dc21

                                      00–022556
                                         CIP

Printed in the United States of America

00 01 02 03 04 05 06 07 QPV 9 8 7 6 5 4 3 2 1

Contents

A Note to the Reader

I often research and write what I need to read. That's certainly the case with this book, not because I haven't pondered the importance of connecting with people, but because I forget too easily. I become too focused on getting a job done—regardless of the concentration and time that job requires. As a result, I find myself tuning out people and other opportunities around me.

Bad move. Selfish habit. Dangerous climate.

Of course, everybody says they love people. What misfit would walk around mumbling, "I hate being around people"? Yet head-hunters insist that the most common—and meaningless—statement on résumés is "have great people skills." After all, what job applicant would tell a prospective employer, "I hate working with other people"?

But saying and doing are two different things.

How about you? Do you really engage others on an intense beam of connection? And I'm not referring simply to having an outgoing personality. Rather, do you routinely make a lasting emotional connection that alters the way others think about themselves, life, and God? Or are you too often distracted with your own concerns?

Life happens while we're thinking about something else. Focusing on the here and now—on those everyday conversations and interactions—causes us to see others, ourselves, and God in a new way. Will you join me in a personal crusade to connect with and influence others so powerfully that we reshape our cracked culture one person at a time?

Dianna Booher

Relationship is probably the most powerful spiritual path that exists in the world today. It's the greatest tool that we have. Our relationships can be the fastest and the most powerful route to the deepest truth, if we know how to use them.

—SHAKTI GAWAIN

Make time to think—it is the source of power.
Make time to play—it is the key to freedom and relaxation.
Make time to read—it is the gateway to knowledge.
Make time to worship—it washes the dust of earth from your eyes.
Make time to help and enjoy friends—no other happiness matches this.
Make time to love—if you don't it will fade away.
Make time to laugh and pray—these two things lighten life's load.
Make time to be alone with God—He is the Source of everything.

—GUARDIAN OF TRUTH

Why Connect?

Darla Duscay knew she was losing blood fast as she hobbled to her back door. Teetering between consciousness and shock, she grabbed a kitchen towel and tightened it around her ankle, then eased herself onto the floor, propping her leg on a chair in an attempt to stop the gushing blood. She could see the bone that had come through the skin. The phone—where was it? She remembered that she'd left it outside beside the ladder that had slipped against the tree and spilled her.

"Alec?" she called to her five-year-old, who was already in bed, along with his two younger brothers. "Alec, I need you to come here."

Her sleepy-eyed son came padding down the hallway. When he saw her, his eyes grew wide.

"Don't be scared, honey. I'm all right, but I need your help. I need you to be brave. Go next door and get the neighbors. Tell them I need help. Quickly."

"I'll be brave, Mommy." Alec dashed out the door.

Moments later the next-door neighbors, who'd moved in only a week earlier, were at Darla's side. Quickly assessing the situation, they called an ambulance and stayed with the children until she was on the way to the hospital. Then they called her best friend. The best friend met her at the hospital, and the friend's husband picked up Darla's three children to keep them through the night and next day.

In the interim, before Darla could get in contact with her husband, who'd gone on a weekend camping trip, friends took charge of all the other details of her life. They kept the children, stayed at her side, and even arranged to have the bloody carpet stains cleaned before she got home from the hospital after surgery. One couple whom she'd met only once at a ball game showed up with lasagna for their dinner.

As Darla later told me this story to explain the awkward boot cast she wore, she summed up this way: "Aren't people great when you need them? People have been so good to me. And you only hear about the bad on TV."

As I listened to her talk about the ordeal that had kept her off the job for weeks and still threatened another surgery, I wondered what would have happened had she not built those connections before she needed them.

Ask any working parent about his or her job or career concerns and eventually you'll hear a wistful comment about lack of support systems when the unusual—measles, Murphy, or a move—happens.

How Did We Get Here from There?

The last century began with unity and ended with isolation. The single most significant change in our culture has been the way we communicate with and relate to each other. And that change has affected our spirits and purposes.

Let me back up a minute. Here's a now-and-then snapshot: Hollywood began the century with the advent of films. Then radio arrived in our homes about twenty years later. Then TV took over at midcentury. Personal computers and the Internet have dominated the last decade.

Think about how these technological changes have changed the way we spend our waking moments. With motion pictures, we all gathered at the theaters to laugh together. With radio, families collected around the console after dinner to listen to their favorite comedians or hear the latest world news. With TV, we chatted over the backyard fence with neighbors about the latest episodes of *The Honeymooners, I Love Lucy, Father Knows Best, Happy Days, The Brady Bunch,* and *M*A*S*H*.

Today, with over five hundred TV choices and an unlimited Internet, we have no idea what everyone else is watching, reading, or playing every evening (that is, if they're not working on their personal computers at 2:00 A.M.). We no longer share common experiences in our pastimes—much less talk about them. The craze of the TV sitcom *Seinfeld*, before it went off the air, wasn't about Seinfeld, per se. It was about connecting on a common experience, even if for a brief episode at the turn of the millennium.

The typical American watches twenty-eight hours of TV each week. Add to that mix computer time and you understand why we no longer have time for relationships. Even our phone calls and personal letters have given way to e-mail.

In short, we have lost our sense of belonging—to our families and to our community. In a sea of souls, we're alone most of the time. And disconnection takes a toll over time.

We Need to Connect to Be Content

Yes, in times of tragedy, even total strangers come to others' rescue. But what about the tragedies that aren't apparent to an onlooker—internal, emotional upheavals in our lives? And what about times of "ordinariness"? How closely do we connect with people on a day-in, day-out basis? How often do we get below the surface of our "Hi, how are you?" and "Fine, thank you" interactions?

During the TV coverage of celebrity deaths, such as Princess Diana's car accident and John F. Kennedy Jr.'s plane crash, we often hear people who have never met them comment about their sense of loss: "I feel such a connection with the family. I've grown up hearing about them and being a part of their lives." Such comments illustrate that, even from a distance, people long to connect, to hold on to common experiences, to celebrate life and commiserate loss together.

Why is connecting with people so vital to our mental, emotional, and spiritual well-being? Because a woman feels more like a woman when she builds and enjoys relationships. Her contentment comes from connecting with other people. As a result, that inner contentment makes her more creative, energetic, persuasive, and powerful in the lives of those she can influence for good—her family, coworkers, and community.

But the typical woman has so many things vying for her attention that she often misses hearing God's voice through her relationships. In other words, they *compete with,* rather than *reflect,* God's truth. For lack of reflection time, we miss the opportunity to connect others to God's love and resources. And the most important "connection," our daily interaction with God, becomes the source of our power to inspire, mold, and nurture others.

That's certainly the case with brain specialist Dr. Phillip Williams.

Michael Taylor phoned his fiancée, Stephanie Sokolosky, in September of 1998 to say he was having a tingling in his left hand. Being a golfer, he dismissed it as perhaps a pinched nerve. Two weeks later when he phoned his bride-to-be about their plans to fly to San Francisco for the weekend, the left side of his face had become numb. She insisted that they go by the hospital and have it checked out before leaving town.

The news from the doctor on call: "We have found a mass on the front right side of your brain. You need to check in to the hospital to begin more tests tomorrow."

The following Saturday morning, Dr. Williams came into the room with the usual personal questions and chitchat: "How old are you? How did you meet? When's the wedding?" Then he did the more unusual; he asked if he could pray with them. "My wife and I pray every morning for God to bring us those patients that He can help."

That Phillip Williams would be the doctor on call at Presbyterian Hospital was no coincidence. Connecting with a Christian doctor to lead them through the ordeal had been Stephanie and Michael's prayer the evening before. Michael underwent surgery a couple of days later to have an egg-sized, nonmalignant tumor removed from his brain.

The connecting process is much like photosynthesis. As plants take in sunlight to create nourishment, we take in the behavior and words of people. We filter them through our psyches and systems, drawing nourishment and insight from them while discarding the unusable. As plants need the sun, so we need each other.

As we talk, work, and play with others around us, our interactions can lead us to valuable insights about life in general and ourselves in particular. And certainly God can speak to us about our direction and decisions in such encounters.

That was also the case with Jane Smith, a Fayetteville, North Carolina, middle-school teacher. At recess, she commented on the baggy pants one of her students was wearing, against school rules. The fourteen-year-old boy, Michael Carter, responded, "The reason I wear them is because it makes me a little more comfortable while I'm going through dialysis treatment." He went on to tell her about needing a kidney transplant.

"Well, I've got a kidney to give you," his teacher answered.

Michael and his mother didn't think she was serious. She was. On December 17, 1999, she donated a kidney to Michael. Michael's mother, Debra Evans, reported during an interview on *The Today Show* that Jane Smith's sacrifice was an answer to their prayers. She and her church family had been praying for years for a kidney donor, but none of the family members who'd been tested had a match. Jane Smith did.

Host Matt Lauer asked the teacher why she planned to undergo the complex surgery for a student she hardly knew, with no other connection, not even race. Her answer: She'd just come home from a church camp in which they'd talked about love, giving, and sacrifice. God had simply impressed her to do it.

Few of us are so responsive. In fact, we don't often stand close enough to hear that still, small voice. We sometimes become so sure of our own destinations and personal competence that we even relegate God's direction to an afterthought. If you've ever regretted a bad decision because you struck out on a path of your own choosing, you understand my point. God can teach us much through our daily interactions with other people IF—and it's a big if—we take the time to listen, consider, learn, and obey.

That's not to say that relationships are the sum total of a dynamic woman's life. She has places to go, people to see, business to do, money to earn, laws to change. But all these ambitions, goals, and results feel secondary in the still of the night. In her heart of hearts, a woman draws her emotional strength, and sometimes even her physical energy, from her relationships.

We Need to Connect to Keep Our Marriages Intact and Our Kids in Tow

A case in point: CNN recently reported the results of a study that showed the most effective preventive measure against teenage pregnancy in the United States is a close relationship between a teen and her parents. In a word: connection.

We sometimes sync our schedules at home so rigidly that we scurry around for days without having a meaningful conversation with our spouses or our kids, our sisters or our mothers. Have you ever wondered how a preteen could build a bomb in the basement without his parents observing what was going on? Have you ever considered how a husband could carry on an affair for two years without his wife becoming suspicious? Have you ever considered why an elderly father could slowly poison himself with pills rather than face another empty day?

The point is not blame—it's a claim. Our lives have become too busy to emotionally connect on a daily basis with our mates and our kids. When they get "out of sorts" with their circumstances, with us, or with themselves, we're so far away emotionally that our internal radars don't detect the difference in their demeanors. And if we do detect their misery, we don't have time to investigate until it's too late.

It doesn't have to be that way. Emotionally connecting with those we love is more about awareness and intention than skill or drama.

We Need to Connect to Stay Sane and Human

Technology doesn't help.

In our technologically wired world, gadgets and schedules are pushing people further apart. We're sitting behind our computers sending e-mail, answering our phones with a recorder, meeting by videoconference, banking and investing on-line, shopping for clothes and gifts from catalogs, asking our florists to deliver flowers to the hospital, and eating at stand-up bars in malls.

At my local Walgreens pharmacy, I can get my prescription refilled automatically on the sixteenth of each month and *their* phone dials *my* phone to remind me to drive through their pickup window. And what's more, we're *paying* for the privilege to purchase without interacting with another human being!

A client can book me for a keynote or training session without ever having talked to me. They go to our Web site, review and download our brochure, and fill out an e-mail inquiry that's automatically sent to us. Our account executive e-mails them to let them know if the requested date is available and sends a letter to confirm the speaking engagement before I ever phone the client to discuss the program content.

Yes, technology has increased the number of our communications, but it has *decreased* our emotional connections. It has speeded up our communication, but it has slowed down our spiritual involvement. It has broadened our everyday world, but it has limited our intentions. It has expanded our opportunities for influence, but it has distracted us from our message of concern.

We sometimes forget that people are people—that they have feelings, wills, perceptions, needs. In fact, technology can remove people's faces. That's why we have the problem with e-mail flaming—those hostile messages that people send with a touch of the key when someone offends them.

Not too long ago, a computer problem caused our office e-mail service to go down overnight. When service was restored the following day, one of our account executives had an e-mail message waiting from someone who wanted to know how to enroll in our public business writing workshop. He sent her an e-mail with the requested information, apologizing for the day's delay in responding due to the computer glitch. Her response came back in total: "Too late. I've already registered for your competitor's course—people who pay attention to their e-mail!!!!"

The world makes us hard. The longer we live, the more we fight to remain assertive, strong, sharp. And that's good—to a point. Nobody likes to be taken advantage of and mistreated. But in the process of "toughening up our skin" so the knocks of life don't bruise us, we can become callous to those around us.

We Need to Connect to Save Our Country

The impetus to connect is not solely for our personal well-being or the sake of our own families. At the risk of sounding like an alarmist, I'll add a final reason for connecting with those around us: We're fast becoming a society of souls drowning in a sea of insensitivity. More and more people are growing emotionally and spiritually desperate. Violence threatens to rip our country to the core. We've splintered into tiny clusters of individuals, sometimes with only one thing in common—survival.

On September 15, 1999, forty-seven-year-old Larry Gene Ashbrook walked into Wedgwood Baptist Church in Fort Worth, Texas, set off a pipe bomb, and then opened gunfire randomly at the crowd of worshipers. Before he finally sat down on the back pew and put the gun to his own head, he had killed seven people and wounded seven others. According to neighbors, he was "a loner," "unfriendly," "weird," "always angry," "disturbed," "grief-stricken," "disappointed in himself," and "an outcast."

As I watched the local television coverage well into the night, I sat on the floor and cried. Although I knew none of the victims, I cried for our country, for the culture we've created, for the future of my children and grandchildren. This latest act of violence follows a long string of others: Pearl, Mississippi; Jonesboro, Arkansas; Paducah, Kentucky; Edinboro, Pennsylvania; Fayette, Tennessee; Springfield, Oregon; and the Littleton, Colorado school killings. The same violence has exploded in the workplace, with employees killed in mass shootings at Xerox, an Oregon shipyard, and Atlanta's financial district.

When the dust settles on each investigation, the words of the families and peers of the victims and the attackers echo the same observations and conclusions: They were angry; they were envious; they were outcasts; they kept to themselves; they felt left out; they felt life had passed them by; they grieved and didn't know where to turn or how to get help; they hated; they wanted revenge. They wanted out of their pain and out of this life. And most tragically, they took other innocent people with them.

U.S. astronaut Michael Collins once described his view of our innate sense of connection this way: "When you first go up there [in space], you look for your hometown. Then you look for your country. But after a while, all you see is the whole earth."

All of us have to stop seeing only a few of us. We have to see all of us to put a stop to the violence.

We have the power to stop these happenings—if we as individuals and the country have the will. We can change the feeling of alienation among our young people and our adults. We can do it by connecting with them—physically, mentally, emotionally, and spiritually—one on one. One person at a time. One situation at a time. One interaction at a time.

That's the purpose for this book. The brief stories and essays that follow illustrate:

- opportunities to connect with others who need our encouragement, insights, and help;

- situations that reconnect us with our own emotions and longings, that power our own souls by plugging into others day to day— at the supermarket, at the school board meeting, on the subway;

- reflections of encounters with others through which God can speak to us about our own wrong attitudes and need for change in ourselves and in our families.

My mission in collecting these memories is to convey the power of connection—to illustrate the power we have to influence others' attitudes, actions, and eternal destinies through our daily interactions—and their power to influence us. It's not a new idea. If you recall, when Saul was converted on the Road to Damascus, he first "connected" with other believers before he started his own ministry.

And if we learn anything from studying the life of Jesus, we learn of His personal connections with others from all walks of life—even when that connection was only a touch or a look. A genuine connection between two people can replace a lifetime of hurt, helplessness, and hate with conviction, courage, and confidence.

In the process, we heal and complete ourselves.

So as you read these vignettes and thoughts from everyday occurrences, I hope they'll cause you either to smile or cry with recognition about the importance of keeping our own hearts soft and sensitive. Reflective moments on simple truths about small things can connect our spirits and refresh our awareness of God's love, direction, rest, and protection.

And if enough people catch the hope and embrace the cause, we can reshape our communities and our country into a culture that once again respects and cares for the individual. We can strive to plug every person into a source of love and life.

By connecting with others, we gain insight, we feel contentment, and we offer comfort and hope for the future.

The Stranger with a Life in His Luggage

Y ou have a lot of trees back here," I said to Vernon one Sunday afternoon in his backyard after we'd been dating only a few months.

"Yep."

"I thought you were going to be moving shortly?"

"I probably will."

"So how long does it take them to grow—won't you be gone before they're big enough to give you any shade?"

"Probably. But somebody will enjoy them after I'm gone." He moved the hose to a new set of roots. "I always plant trees wherever I live."

"Hmm." Seemed like a waste of time to me. I enjoy gardening about as much as I love to scrub a dirty skillet.

"Did I tell you about the man who helped me set all these trees out?"

I shook my head, and he related the following story.

Vernon watched as the old man relished his fried chicken, occasionally dabbing at the corners of his mouth with his napkin. The mom-and-pop restaurant drew only locals, even for Sunday lunch. In his single days, Vernon often stopped there to grab a bite of lunch on his way home from church. It was the kind of place where the owners call you by name and remember that you like gravy on the side.

His battered suitcase under the table beside him, the elderly diner had apparently walked from the bus station across the street. Vernon noticed that the old man had finished his lunch but didn't seem to be in any hurry to leave. He lingered over his glass of water, simply watching other diners as they came and went, occasionally moving his suitcase from side to side to prevent people from tripping as they passed among the tightly arranged tables. He seemed amused by the children who were flying paper airplanes over their food as their parents coaxed them to eat. The twinkle in his eye seemed to reveal memories of family days gone by.

Always intrigued by people with stories to tell, Vernon took his last swig of iced tea and said to the older man across the narrow aisle, "Are you visiting someone here in Kingwood?"

"No. Just passing through."

"Where are you from?"

"Philadelphia." He paused for a moment, as if to assess Vernon's real interest in his itinerary. Obviously deciding Vernon's interest was genuine, he elaborated. "My wife died a few weeks ago. Been married fifty-two years. Decided I needed a change. Got all my belongings here in this case." He patted the bent brown bag as if it were a collie. "Yeah, going out to live with my son."

That much information in such a brief exchange was just the kind of thing my husband needed to build a two-hour conversation. Although women are often said to have special antennas for collecting information, Vernon does an admirable job himself. The old man's response was one of those thumbnail sketches that wallop you up beside the head with the same kind of impact you sometimes get from a novel or movie.

As Vernon later related the incident to me, I could hear a leftover hint of sadness in his voice when he explained, "So I asked the old man to come home with me for the afternoon."

"You—what? A total stranger?"

"He had nowhere else to go."

So that Sunday in the restaurant he had said to the old man dining at the next table, "Where's your son live?"

"He's out in San Diego—or somewhere near there. That's where he's meeting my bus."

"Nice place." Vernon finished his tea and started to get up to pay his check. "So are you going to walk around here and see a little of the city before you go? There're some great walking trails near here."

The old man shook his head.

"So what time does your bus leave?"

"Ten o'clock tonight."

"You've got to wait nine hours?"

"Bus is not the best way to travel, I guess. But it's cheap," the old man smiled, not at all bitterly.

"So why don't you come on home with me for the afternoon, and I'll bring you back to catch your bus at ten o'clock? That's too long for you to have to sit here and wait."

The old man seemed to search Vernon's face for sincerity. "I wouldn't want to impose. I could just sit here another couple hours and then mosey on back over to the bus station."

"No, that won't be comfortable. I don't live far away. Got a little garden. I wasn't planning on doing anything special—just planting a few trees. I could use some help."

The old man's face lit up. "Oh, now that—yeah, I could help you do that. I know about planting trees." And with that, he reached for his suitcase and followed Vernon out of the restaurant.

Once in the backyard, after Vernon had given him some of his own old work clothes to change into, the old man seemed much younger. "If you want some advice, I'd tell you to stagger those trees," he said as Vernon was about to dig the second hole.

"What do you mean?"

"Like this." The visitor took the extra shovel and began to mark the spots across the lawn. When he returned to where Vernon was standing, he told him the reason: "The roots don't crowd each other, and the resulting shade from the canopy will be wider."

"I see," Vernon said appreciatively. "Nobody ever told me that before. Makes sense. Let's do it then."

They set out nine trees before dark. In between, they spread their lives.

When they'd finished, Vernon showed him to the extra shower so he could clean up and change back into his traveling clothes. He took him out for dinner on the way back to the bus station for his ten o'clock departure. As they parted, they exchanged phone numbers and vowed to keep in touch.

But Vernon never heard from the man again.

Four years later, Vernon received a letter from the old man's son, telling him that his father had recently passed away. The letter said in part, "My father never stopped talking about you and your kindness to him that Sunday afternoon. He was truly amazed that in this day and time you would invite him, a stranger, into your home—and make him feel useful. That was the best part. I found your address in his room and thought I should let you know what your kindness meant to him. He talked of you and that day often, as if you were old friends."

As Vernon related the story to me while watering the saplings spread across his lawn, I understood that they had indeed been friends—even if for only a day. Friendship may be more appropriately measured in intensity than longevity.

In Jesus' words to his disciples I think he was making the same distinction that Vernon conveyed when he invited the old man to join him. "I no longer call you servants . . . Instead, I have called you friends" (John 15:15). The distinction provides context and reason for those brief encounters along life's way.

■ ■ ■

The idea of strictly minding our own business is moldy rubbish. Who could be so selfish?

—MYRTIE BARKER

Spare moments are the gold dust of time—of all the portions of our life, the spare minutes are the most fruitful in good or evil.

—UNKNOWN

Blessed are those who can give without remembering and take without forgetting.

—PRINCESS ELIZABETH ASQUITH BIBESCO

One can never pay in gratitude; one can only pay "in kind" somewhere else in life.

—ANNE MORROW LINDBERG

In My Dreams, You Were Not There

At 2:00 A.M., my husband woke up in a cold sweat. He reached over to touch me and said simply, "You're here." I roused only slightly, heard him pad down the hallway toward the kitchen, and went back to sleep.

Later when I pulled into my parking spot at work, I saw him through the window, waiting in my office. Although we work together in our business, we leave the house at different times in the morning and have different schedules each day. As soon as I stepped inside my office, he took me in his arms and whispered, "I'm so glad you're here."

When he finally released me, he said, "I had a terrible dream last night. I couldn't get it out of my mind. I kept waking up in a cold sweat. I tried getting up and walking around, but every time I went back to sleep, the dream just kept going. So finally I got up and stayed up the rest of the night."

One look at his tired eyes and ashen face confirmed his lack of sleep.

"I dreamed that you were in a McDonald's restaurant, and there was a random shooting, and somebody called me to come identify you. And there were these bodies everywhere on the floor, covered with coats and blankets. I was frantic, yanking up the coats, hoping I wouldn't find you." His voice grew more urgent as he continued to describe the dream, and his eyes filled with tears. "And I kept running from one police officer to the next, telling them maybe you weren't there after all. I was running into the rest room and back outside to your car, trying to find you—everywhere but on that floor . . . It was the most horrible dream."

He held me tightly in his arms and repeated, "But you're here. I'm so glad you're here."

The dream bothered him for two days. It had been generated, we felt sure, by our late-night discussion just before falling off to sleep. Our conversation had centered on my forty-eight-year-old brother, Keith, who had recently been diagnosed with cancer.

Tolstoy wrote, "All happy families are alike, but each unhappy family is unhappy in its own way." As Keith and I were growing up, our happy family did all the routine things happy families do. Our parents watched us play our basketball, football, and baseball games. We routinely traveled to visit grandparents to eat pumpkin pie, fried chicken, homemade bread, and goulash that had simmered for hours. We built tree houses with our cousins. We played tag until somebody skinned a knee and had to go inside for a Band-Aid. We took vacations, attended parties, and sang around campfires. We argued over who would sit by the window on long trips and who caused whom to spill the Coke on the carpet.

The routineness of our happy childhood had perhaps dulled its importance in our lives as adults.

Keith and I sat in his hospital room wondering what had happened to our connection as brother and sister. To outsiders, ours still looked like a close relationship. We talk by phone every few weeks; we gather around our parents' table for birthday and holiday meals; we exchange Christmas gifts and birthday cards; we visit in each other's homes a few times a year and play a game of forty-two now and then. We take an interest in each other's children's lives—passing around baby clothes and secondhand furniture for college apartments.

"You and I haven't really stayed in touch all these years," he said to me from his hospital bed.

At first, I was surprised, even hurt, at the comment. Was he saying that he couldn't feel my concern through his ordeal? How could that be? I'd visited. I'd sent cards. I'd phoned every day of his hospitalization. I'd prayed daily and told him so.

But as I watched his tears fall and felt my own trickle down my face, I decided that he was right. We had not connected our hearts in a long time. Instead, we had been going through the family rituals, skimming along on the surface of life, without watching and bracing for the waves.

That night as we sat in the falling darkness in his hospital room, facing his uncertain future, we shared our souls—our dreams, our regrets, our fears, and our pain—not as children but as adults. As we talked, I began to see anew the heart of this gentle man, my brother, as if I were seeing him for the first time.

My thoughts rolled back to the year I married and moved away from home as he moved off to college. When my husband and I brought our first baby home to my parents for weekend visits, Keith, still a single man of twenty, swept him up in his arms and chucked his chin. As Jeff grew from a toddler to a teen and even as Keith married and had toddlers of his own, he was never too busy to take my two to get ice cream, to play catch on the nearby ball field, or to let them drive his car in preparation for earning their own.

As a father of teens, he judged debate contests, fed 4-H calves, and took his turn staffing snow-cone concession stands.

As a husband, he welcomed his in-laws for extended visits, waited on his wife's elderly aunt while she recuperated from hip surgery, and took in a brother-in-law who was going through a divorce.

As a church member, he befriended the pastor and put in his yard, hosted youth parties around his swimming pool, and for years changed baby diapers and read stories in the church nursery.

In his spare time, he had landscaped half his city. With his own landscape business as a moonlighting hobby, he offered his services free of charge to nonprofits in the neighborhood: his children's schools, the churches, the recreational centers.

In recent years, when my husband and I decided to move back to Dallas from Houston, he took two days off work to drive us all over the metroplex, offering his recommendations on where to buy land and build our house. And once the builder had worked his magic and we'd moved in, he used his remaining week of vacation to help us put in our yard and sprinkler system.

How long had it been since I'd seen my brother through these eyes?

During his fourth week of daily radiation treatments, I phoned one evening about bedtime to ask how he was feeling. My sister-in-law answered. "He's pretty tired, all right. The doctor said these mega-doses would almost wipe him out every day. And he's still trying to work six hours a day."

"If he's still awake, let me say hello to him," I said.

"Actually, he's not here. He's gone over to visit Mrs. Stephens for a few minutes," my sister-in-law explained. I recognized the name of an elderly widow who'd been a friend of our parents. "He put in some flower beds for her a few weeks ago. And he just wanted to check on her and see if she needed anything else."

So like him. Is this the same brother with whom I've so lightly shared daily and weekly rituals? Why have I taken his being there for me and with me so much for granted? Why do we understand the fragility of life only when we're about to lose it? Now in the face of death, we have taken the time to discuss our lives. We have cried together, reconnected our hearts, examined our souls, and sorted out our responsibilities and plans for the future. In the grip of death, we see each other more clearly.

Rituals need to ripen into reality shared at the center of our being. As with my husband's dream, often we need the reassuring physical touch of a loved one to say, "You're here. I'm so glad you're here."

■ ■ ■

When we die we leave behind us all that we have and take with us all that we are.

—UNKNOWN

I am the resurrection and the life. He who believes in me will live, even though he dies; and whoever lives and believes in me will never die.

—JOHN 11:25–26

You never realize death until you realize love.

—KATHARINE BUTLER HATHAWAY

Paint by Numbers

The bathroom would have been easier had we not decided to take it in shifts. But shift work is better than no work, and getting five couples together on the same weekend had been no easy task.

It all started when a Realtor friend mentioned to our Bible-study group that a client of hers needed to sell her house. The woman's husband had left her, she was feeling overwhelmed, and she could no longer afford the house payments. She wanted to sell the house as soon as possible and move into a cheaper apartment. The Realtor, Karen, and her husband, Paul, had already spent a Saturday helping the woman mow the grass and clean up the debris enough to stake a "For Sale" sign in the front yard.

After their call for help, our group decided to make the house our project. Our work plan included repainting the master bathroom and bedroom and repairing the backyard fence that was about to collapse. As the various couples volunteered their time for the next weekend, it was quickly apparent that we would have difficulty making ourselves available at exactly the same hours. So we quickly divided the chores among couples and decided to show up whenever we could the following weekend.

Turning into the cul-de-sac, we couldn't mistake the house we were to work on. The front of the small lot looked more like an overgrown field than a yard in the suburbs. Karen and Paul had already cut dead limbs from trees, trimmed out-of-control shrubs that sprawled higher than the fence, and pulled flowering weeds that were choking out the grass. They hung up their work gloves with a promise to return the next day to finish the job.

I got out my paintbrushes and headed inside to find Lisa and Alex at work in the bathroom. He was painting the trim in the master closet; she was removing the light fixtures over the mirrors. I poured paint in my pan, dipped my roller in the thick, soup-like latex, and announced my plan to take the south wall.

For the first half-hour, we talked. Jobs. Kids. Upcoming seminars. Quirky coworkers. People in the news. Someone from the fence-repair detail showed up with soft drinks and pizza. We ate, laughed, talked. Then back to the ladders and paint.

It took only about two hours for the project to turn into real work. Alex and Lisa had to leave, and I took on the bathroom detail alone. That's when I began to notice how much remained to be done. As I scraped the wall behind the toilet bowl, I became a little irritated. I had to put down my pan and brush and get a rag to wash off the cob-webs before I could finish painting. Although tempted just to paint over the dirt and dust on the wall, I knew better. So I stopped to pre-pare the walls as I'd learned in Wall-Painting 101 years earlier as a newlywed. Didn't the homeowner know that you can't just paint over dirt? I guessed not. Oh, well.

As my arm started to ache, I grew more agitated. Every few min-utes I had to climb off the ladder, put down the pan, and move some-thing out of the way so I wouldn't chance dripping paint on it. There was the hair dryer, still plugged in and left out on the bathroom counter. Hadn't the woman known this was the weekend our group was coming to help her whip this house into shape and get it into sell-ing condition? Sure, she had. Karen said she often worked weekends as a nurse. Even so, I had expected her to be around—if not to help with the work herself, at least to express gratitude that someone had come to her aid.

I climbed down the ladder again and tried to clear the next section of the bathroom counter. Hair clips. Opened tubes of lipstick and mascara. Wet washcloth. Couldn't she at least have put her things in the drawers, out of our way? Surely she didn't expect that to be part of the paint job. The whole job would have gone so much faster if I didn't have to continually stop to move or clean something.

As I crawled back onto the counter and tried to maneuver the paintbrush around the towel bar, I could see that I was about to make a big mess. Where was that screwdriver? I found a clean place to deposit the paint pan and removed the rest of the bathroom hardware so that I could paint under it.

By the time I finished, I realized that this two-hour project had turned into six. With aching arms and shoulders, I finished the last of the trim and gathered up my brushes. Loaded with drop cloth and pans, I started out through the bedroom and caught my foot in the hose of the vacuum cleaner. Luckily, I landed on my feet. Why was the vacuum in the middle of the floor? And why was the ironing board set up on the other side of the bed?

I strained to keep my judgments in check. After all, maybe she'd had to work double shifts for days on end. Maybe her kids had been sick all week. Maybe she'd hardly had time to get them up, fed, dressed, and to a baby-sitter before having to be back at work. Not mine to judge.

Washing my paintbrushes under the faucet in the backyard, I glanced through the window to the family room. It looked dark, dingy, and depressing inside. I called out to Alan, working alongside my husband as they replaced boards in the fence, "Has either one of you seen a bucket or something that I could use to wash out these brushes?"

"Yeah. Inside the garage," Don answered me from behind as he and Charlene walked up the driveway. "We were over yesterday helping with the yard work, and a guy brought out that plastic dishpan there."

"Good. Thanks." I picked up the dishpan he'd pointed to and piled the brushes into it to soak a few minutes. "What guy are you talking about?"

"I think it must have been her son," Don said. "He looked about eighteen or twenty years old."

"She has a teenage son? The woman who lives here?" I asked incredulously.

Don nodded. "Yes. And a teenage daughter."

"Are you sure?"

"Yep. They sat inside and watched TV all yesterday afternoon while we were out working on the lawn. One of them came out and watched us a few minutes, then went back inside. Said he was going to the store for a Coke and then came back after a few minutes. Went back inside and stayed there until we left about dark."

I swished the brushes in the water. Figures. Dirty bathroom. Hair dryer and lipstick in my way. What a waste of time. I began to think of a thousand things I could have been doing around my house in the same six hours. What nerve—asking us to help her when she had two able-bodied teens underfoot.

My husband and Alan finished replacing the last rotten board in the fence, and we began to sort through hammers, saws, mowers, saw-horses, and rags to go our separate ways. As we drove away from the house, I caught a glimpse of the newly manicured lawn in the rearview mirror. Had it been a waste of time? Had the woman living there, whom we'd never even met, really needed the help? Had we asked our friends to give up their weekend for someone who had misrepresented the situation and was taking advantage of others' generosity?

My put-upon attitude served only to remind me how far I was from understanding the concept of self-sacrificing service. And that realization made me uneasy for the rest of the afternoon.

But within weeks, long after the ache in my painting arm had subsided, I noticed several things. Don and Charlene seemed to feel a part of our group as never before. Alan and my husband shared aspects of themselves that they'd never known and appreciated about each other before the fencing. Alex and Lisa have commented on the fun of their first home-painting project as a couple. Karen has become a successful Realtor with a reputation for caring about her clients' total needs.

You've probably heard the principle applied to God and our money: He doesn't need it, but we need to give it. I don't know whether the family with a home to sell really needed our help that weekend. But we needed to give it. Muscles of generosity that are not exercised regularly grow flabby and weak.

■ ■ ■

If someone listens or stretches out a hand or whispers a word of encouragement or attempts to understand a lonely person, extraordinary things begin to happen.

—LORETTA GIRZARTIS

What you want to be eventually, that you must be every day; and by and by the quality of your deeds will get down into your soul.

—FRANK CRANE

All Happy Families

Nick Irons swam 1,550 miles down the Mississippi River to win the distinction that earned him the Freedom Medal. Why? Because he loves his dad, who's suffering from multiple sclerosis. The marathon swim was Nick's idea to draw attention to the disease and raise money for research that he hopes will result in a cure in time to help his father.

As twenty-something Nick and I met in my office to work on his acceptance speech, I listened to him talk about the obstacles and challenges he'd faced. But I also listened between the lines as he painted a picture of his relationship with his parents and his brother.

All happy families, Nick's included, share common attributes and experiences.

Nick's swim down the Mississippi came about because of his love, admiration, and respect for his parents. It would be difficult to separate the three ingredients of this recipe. Nick tells about hatching the idea while away at college. His idea was to attempt some amazingly challenging physical feat—one that would generate plenty of media attention and money for his cause. But had there been only love, he might not have been successful. At an age when most young people feel quite capable of taking on the world alone, Nick had enough admiration and respect for his parents to know that he needed their feedback and endorsement before he went forward with his idea.

Speaking of the proposal he'd written outlining his idea and plan, he said, "I called to tell them I had an idea. They tried to get me to tell them about it on the phone, but I wanted to do it in person. I wanted to see their reaction to it—for real." He needed to see their acceptance and approval.

"My dad read it, and tears came to his eyes. He didn't say anything for a long time. Then he just handed it to my mom. And she went off into the bedroom to read it alone. Then she came back and just kept walking around the room, saying, 'Whoa. Whoa. Whoa.' She said 'whoa' with just about every inflection and volume you can think of." Nick went on to explain, "It was really very important that they agreed and were behind me on this."

Why? I asked myself as I considered this very determined and physically capable young man standing before me. Because members of happy families need to know that their families support them.

Love is seldom enough. Sometimes love between parent and child expresses itself in weak, compulsive, and even hurtful ways. In happy families, however, love mixed with approval and support sustains family members in a way that allows them to overcome enormous obstacles and meet extraordinary challenges.

Another ingredient in happy families is their willingness to connect as a single unit and move toward a common goal. To support Nick's goal to swim the Mississippi, each family member had an assigned role. His father mapped out the journey for each day's schedule and secured hotel rooms and meals along the way. His mother took on the public relations job, pitching their story to reporters to gain media coverage. His brother followed him in a small boat as he swam, carrying supplies and offering moral support during punishing rainstorms and heat waves.

Nick recalls a time he had been in the water for a couple of hours when a rainstorm developed. At first, it was refreshing. Then it began to rain so hard that he couldn't see where he was going or hear his brother's voice yelling at him to stop. With each stroke, he was swallowing water and trying to catch a glimpse of what was ahead. Finally he swam right into the side of the boat and cut his head.

On another day in a different rainstorm, his brother's boat capsized in the waves. Nick had to turn around and swim several hundred yards backward to help his brother get back in the boat. At one point, he became so tired of swimming in the rain against the waves that his brother feared for his safety. His brother pulled his boat up beside him and begged him to stop and rest.

"I can't," Nick called back. "If I get out now, I know I'll never get back in the water." With that realization, he pushed away from the side of the boat and swam another two and a half hours.

They had a goal. Each family member played his or her part in reaching it.

As I visualized Nick fighting in that rainstorm and felt the weariness of his aching arms taking the next stroke and the next stroke and the next, I reflected on other happy families I'd known who'd pulled together as a team to achieve a common goal. The Millards, friends of our family since childhood, had pulled together as the mother decided to get a college degree in her midthirties. For three years, the father and two kids took on extra chores and demanded less of her time so she could devote the necessary hours to study. Another family, acquaintances of ours, moved to Houston for three years so the eleven-year-old daughter could work with a special coach to accomplish her goal of competing in the Olympics. Adult brothers and sisters work together for months, sometimes years, to rotate their schedules and vacation days to care for elderly parents.

Happy families work together toward a common goal.

Happy families also laugh together. Even in the midst of their pain, they find things that amuse them. They share a pleasant outlook to cheer each other through doubt and the demands of duty.

One of the things that amused Nick during months of swimming four to six hours a day was the fact that he had recurring dreams of sleeping! He dreamed of dying and going to heaven—to sleep on a big feather bed. Falling asleep even in restaurants as he sat down to eat, he felt that he never got enough rest before having to crawl back into the water.

Food became another funny subject. Nick began to lose weight. He started the swim weighing 215 pounds and ended the ordeal at less than 180. As Nick tells it, he got so skinny that his brother, Andy, started calling him Twig Boy. And Twig Boy wasn't an epithet he wanted to keep. Things improved in the southern part of the country. He had biscuits and gravy for breakfast. Fried chicken for lunch. Steak and barbecue for dinner. According to Nick, he considered holding up a sign: "Will swim the Mississippi for food!" Just thinking of that prospect while in the water, he began to laugh so hard that he almost drowned.

Laughter and the sound of family voices around the dinner table will keep more teens off the streets at night than the strictest curfew.

As Nick and I worked on the final segment of his story during our coaching day, he told about the victory scene—the moment he swam ashore at Baton Rouge and was greeted by several high school and college marching bands and thirty or forty reporters. His dad, still able to walk with his cane, had come to meet him as he swam ashore for the final time. His mom had spent weeks talking with skeptical reporters, trying to entice them to cover the story of this family's fund-raising efforts.

Nick pushed his way through the throng of waiting media into his dad's arms. "Happy birthday, Dad. I love you. I did it for you."

Happy families express their love openly. They're vocal about it— at awards banquets, at weddings and funerals, at the dinner table. They understand that no one holds a guarantee for tomorrow, so they express their feelings today. In front of bosses, clients, neighbors, friends, and community, family members welcome the opportunity to tell themselves and others that their family relationships take first priority over other concerns.

Nick's acceptance of the Freedom Medal connects us all once again to that snugly feeling generated by a loving family. Families of faith, especially, fit together faster and firmer than most.

■ ■ ■

Silent gratitude isn't much use to anyone.

—GLADYS BROWYN STERN

If you cannot get rid of the family skeleton, you may as well make it dance.

—GEORGE BERNARD SHAW

No matter how much you disagree with your kin, if you are a thoroughbred you will not discuss their shortcomings with the neighbors.

—Tom Thompson

The best Christmas gift of all is the presence of a happy family all wrapped up with one another.

—Unknown

The family altar would alter many a family.

—Unknown

Which Way from Witchcraft?

In New York City, I hopped into a taxi driven by a man from Haiti. "Where are you coming from?" he asked.

"From Miami tonight, but I'm from Dallas." I answered the rather routine question absent-mindedly as I settled in for the half-hour ride before what I hoped would be a good night's sleep.

"Great. That's where I plan to get a job—Dallas or Miami—as soon as possible."

"What kind of job are you looking for?"

"Something in either human resources or the import-export business."

"Hmm." My ears perked up. A coincidence?

He elaborated, "For years, I didn't have a degree because I didn't think I could afford college. When I came here to your country, I went through a battery of tests with several agencies. They told me I had a high IQ. So I was able to get a few entry-level jobs in the HR field. But I decided I wanted that degree; you know what I mean?"

I nodded as he glanced toward the backseat. He spoke impeccable English, with the syntax of an educated person.

"I got a degree in business administration and learned to speak four languages. I figure that prepares me to go in either direction."

Suddenly, he switched the radio from a Christian station to a classical station.

"No, that's fine. No need to change stations. I'm a Christian myself."

At that, he took his hands off the wheel, lifted them toward heaven, and said, "Thank you, Lord." He turned back to me. "I was just sitting here, reading my Bible," he paused to pull it from under the seat as if to prove what he was saying. "I was praying that God would send me someone to help me move to Dallas or Miami. I have to move away to establish a new life for my family."

I had been interested up to this point; now I was totally intrigued as he told me his story.

"I'm a Christian, and I come from a strong Christian home in Haiti. When I came to the United States, I could not find a wife. So my family arranged my marriage to a Haitian woman, as is our custom. She came here, we met for the first time, and we married. Although our families knew each other, my parents didn't know that my wife practiced witchcraft. And we were already married before I discovered this. For many, many years now, I have tried to win her to Christianity."

I interrupted his story to ask, "Why is she so resistant?"

"I don't know. Witchcraft has hardened her heart. She has changed so much over the years since she has become so involved with her cult here in New York."

Then he continued with his wife's story. "She had worked for ten years with one company and then lost her job—through no fault of her own. She didn't—still doesn't—have a very glamorous job. She is a maid for a hotel chain. She was very honest at this job. Once she found a wallet full of cash and turned it in. She even found a diamond ring in a toilet and turned it in. Many of her supervisors praised her for these things, her honesty. Then she got a new supervisor, who wanted to hire one of his friends for the job. So he accused my wife of stealing."

"Did she?"

"No. It was a silly situation. Her supervisor accused her of leaving the hotel with a plate of cookies left over after a conference. She told the new supervisor that the big boss had given her permission to take home leftover food, but the supervisor fired her anyway. He thought since she was a foreigner, she wouldn't do anything about it. Then I came home one evening and found her sitting in the middle of the floor, crying. It broke my heart to see her so unhappy. I wasn't aware that she was so unhappy not to have her own job. She told me that since she'd been asking her own gods to help her get another job, she didn't understand why she couldn't find one.

"So I thought, here is my opportunity to win her to Christianity. I told her I would strike a bargain with her: I said to her that night, 'If I call on my God to help you find a job, will you believe in him and convert to Christianity?' And she agreed.

"My studies in HR and business administration had given me some understanding of the legal issues of her termination. So the next day, I wrote a letter on her behalf to her own company and threatened legal action. Within two days, she got a call from the hotel chain hiring her back 'temporarily.' And she was the only one they hired back from several they'd fired. And then we had to go through arbitration. We won the case against the hotel, and she got her job back permanently. But this whole waiting process took a long time."

At this point in his story, I assumed we had come to a happy ending, but then I remembered his earlier comment about having to establish a new life. I asked, "So did she convert to your God?"

He shook his head sadly. "After we won the case, the first thing I said was, 'Let's get on our knees to thank God.' But she refused. The first thing she wanted to do on her first vacation was fly back to Haiti to be with her family and thank her own gods."

He paused for a moment, glancing toward the backseat again, looking straight into my eyes. "I can't go on. It is breaking my heart to see how she's raising our kids. She's still practicing witchcraft and trying to teach them. Although they are still very young, they don't know which way to go. I have to move them all away from here—either to Dallas or Miami to get a job and start over in a new place away from her friends and the cult here."

I nodded that I understood.

"Can you help me?"

As he had been relating his story, I had become slowly aware that God himself had put me in that cab that night. I'd just come from Miami where I was speaking at a convention. At dinner I had been seated next to the CEO of the largest import-export company in the country. Our lengthy conversation had focused on how difficult it was for his company to find multilingual employees.

I held out the CEO's business card to the taxi driver. "Tell him I told you to call about his need for multilingual employees." I also wrote down the name of some colleagues among my HR associates in Dallas in case things didn't work out in Miami.

But as I stepped out of the taxi at midnight, I had a strong feeling that he wouldn't be needing those.

■ ■ ■

There are two ways of spreading light—to be the candle or the mirror that reflects it.

—UNKNOWN

I do not pray for success, I ask for faithfulness.

—MOTHER TERESA

Providence has at all times been my dependence, for all other resources seem to have failed us.

—GEORGE WASHINGTON

God's providence is not in baskets lowered from the sky, but through the hands and hearts of those who love him. The lad without food and without shoes made the proper answer to the cruel-minded woman who asked, "But if God loves you, wouldn't he send you food and shoes?" The boy replied, "God told someone, but he forgot."

—GEORGE A. BUTTRICK

Cheerleader Blues

Leading the workshop proved difficult that afternoon. It wasn't that I couldn't be passionate about teaching systems engineers to write good documentation. It was the suspense of waiting to learn the outcome of the elections back home. My fifteen-year-old daughter was trying out for cheerleader of her sophomore class.

But not without reluctance. Although she seldom met a stranger in her day-to-day interactions, making herself vulnerable to the outcome of a popularity vote by the student body took guts. At least, that's what I'd said to her when she had discussed with me the pros and cons of trying out.

"But, Mom, this isn't like back in your day when you could just get out there and yell and jump around and if everybody liked you, you got it. You have to be able to do stuff."

"Like what?" I wanted to know. This wasn't the time to get sidetracked by an intergenerational stanza of "Back in my day, I had to walk five miles to school, in the snow, without a coat, uphill both ways."

"Like you've got to be good at gymnastics, for one thing," she continued.

"So? You took gym. You can do flips."

"Yeah, but I'm not as good as some of the rest of them—everybody else has been taking gym since they were four." I doubted that generalization but let it pass to concentrate on the bigger message she was trying to communicate—her lack of self-confidence as she approached this latest goal. "I still can't do the splits like Amy Taylor."

"Well, you can practice before tryouts."

"Do you really think I can do it? Do you think I should? Do you want me to?"

"Sure you can do it. But I don't care if you try out or not. It's not what *I* want. It's what *you* want. If you want to be a cheerleader, you should set that as your goal and start to work."

She had—for three solid weeks. She had come home every day, done her homework, and then bounced out to the backyard to tumble till it hurt.

I flipped off the projector promptly at five, said good-bye to my IBM engineering students, and rushed to the bank of telephones in the hotel lobby to dial home. She picked up the phone on the first ring.

"Well, did you win?" I gushed into the phone, my heart in my throat.

Her barely audible "hello" turned into a sob halfway through the "no."

"Oh, honey, I'm so sorry."

She couldn't speak. I heard only jerky sniffles in response.

"You must feel awful."

This only made her cry more loudly and openly. I've never been so frustrated by having to be away from home overnight as I was that night. I hated the way the scheduling had turned out—I was home on Friday when the winners were to have been announced, but a clear-cut winner hadn't emerged on the first ballot. Four girls had tied for the two sophomore spots, and my daughter had made it to the runoffs. Unfortunately, the runoff would be held the day I had to be away. Good news we could share by phone. Bad news called for closer contact. Listening to the disappointment in her tone that afternoon, I thought my heart would break.

"So when did they announce the results? Second period or at the end of the day?"

"Just before the final bell. Mom, I was so embarrassed."

"Tell me about it. What happened?"

"I just lost, that's all. Amy Taylor won. I didn't do the jumps that well."

I tried to get her to talk so that by sharing her frustration, I could lighten her disappointment. It didn't seem to be helping.

"But look at it this way: At least you made the runoffs. Only four of you got that far."

She only sniffled louder.

"Honey, I'm so sorry I'm not there."

"I can't go to school tomorrow, Mom. I'll be so embarrassed. Only two of us are the losers. How can I go to school tomorrow?" She sobbed louder as if her heart would break. "How can I ever go back?"

It wasn't a question, so I didn't try to answer it. "Is your brother there?"

"Yes."

"Put him on a minute."

When her older brother came to the phone, I intended to give him a "bury the hatchet" talk about petty sibling rivalry and to ask him to be my arms and heart for his sister that evening. The appeal to his brotherly concern wasn't necessary.

"I told her, Mom, that she was the best one. That all of us seniors were hoping she'd get it. If the juniors and seniors had gotten to vote, she'd have won. And I told her she should be glad she's on the student council—that's better anyway. They're the real leaders of the school."

I thanked him for supporting his sister, and he volunteered to stay home and "be there for her" for the rest of the evening. He then put Lisa back on the phone.

Her voice was barely above a whisper. "I just can't go to school tomorrow, Mom. Everybody will tease me for losing."

"No, honey, they won't. They won't tease about that."

"Mom, I just can't help it," she sobbed. "I can't help feeling jealous."

I understood the feeling and the pain.

"They'll all feel sorry for me. And all my friends will be talking about it, and I'll start to cry in front of them. What can I say?" Her voice broke again.

I tried again. "They won't tease you, honey. They'll admire you for having the courage to try out. How many other girls do you think want to be cheerleaders?"

"I don't know," she seemed to pause to think about it. "I guess most of them."

"And how many had the courage to try out?"

"Sixty."

"And how many made it to the final round?"

She started crying again. "I'm never going to try out for anything like that ever again."

"Well, you may change your mind after you've had time to think about it. You set your mind to do something—to try out—and you did it. That isn't failure. You can do the splits now. You made new friends. You know more people. More people know you."

She started to sob again. I felt as if I were dipping into a deep well, trying to pull out a bucket of comfort. With no luck. I couldn't think of a single thing to do or say to ease her disappointment, the first of many disappointments that no doubt would come her way.

A line of people had formed behind me, waiting for the phone. I promised to call her back in an hour to see if she felt better. Feeling as though I were imprisoned on a remote island off the coast of Africa, I went to my hotel room and waited. I called back an hour later. She was no longer sobbing. When I commented that she sounded as though she felt a little better, the tears started again. We talked another half-hour. I called again at bedtime. The sobs had subsided to sniffles. I called the next morning at six o'clock. She had decided to go to school after all.

The initial embarrassment that seemed for a fifteen-year-old like an overwhelming tidal wave had passed by the time I got home that evening. In its place was quiet acceptance. We sat on the couch, and I held her in my arms for a long time that evening. With my rocking, I offered comfort for all the future hurts from which I knew I'd never be able to protect her. The loss of boyfriends. An unfair or insensitive professor. Serious illness. Career disappointments. The death of a friend. The loss of beloved grandparents.

In such moments between parent and child, we catch a tiny glimpse of God's own love and concern for us, his children, when we hurt.

I am beginning to learn that it is the sweet, simple things of life which are the real ones after all.

—LAURA INGALLS WILDER

Sharing is sometimes more demanding than giving.

—MARY CATHERINE BATESON

And I pray that you, being rooted and established in love, may have power, together with all the saints, to grasp how wide and long and high and deep is the love of Christ.

—EPHESIANS 3:17–18

If Memory Serves Me Right—and It Rarely Does

Some years ago, while visiting Universal Studios in Orlando, we toured the *I Love Lucy* exhibit, a room devoted to Lucille Ball and Desi Arnaz memorabilia. Three separate screens played excerpts of their 1950s sitcom. As small groups of people stood in front of the big-screen TVs, we could hear them squeal with delight, "Look at this one. Remember Lucy stomping the grapes in that winery? And look, that's when she got sunburned. She looks like a penguin, waddling around in those towels. Ooh, look. Remember when she was pregnant? I remember that one. Little Ricky. Don't you remember? I do."

And these are the same people who can't remember where they put their car keys each morning!

What fascinates me is my memory's unpredictability. A random comment in a business meeting can trigger the memory of an argument with a coworker two years earlier, yet I can't remember whether I unplugged the iron before leaving for work that morning. My granddaddy could remember how many cattle he sold to Uncle Jack in 1948 in exchange for the house and barn on his land, but he couldn't remember why he was taking the heart medicine that had been prescribed two weeks earlier.

But this memory madness isn't necessarily related to age. Kids can remember stunts from Brady Bunch reruns, but they can't remember what homework was assigned the day before yesterday. They can remember the 972 e-mail addresses and phone numbers of their closest friends, but they can't remember to take out the garbage on Thursdays.

Case in point: When both my kids were home from college over the holidays one year, one said to the other, "You remember how much fun we used to have building forts with blankets at the top of the stairs?" Who's he kidding? I played referee while they took turns tattling on each other. Fun? Maybe he's remembering another sister, another lifetime?

Another puzzling feature of memory is how much better things look from the distance of time. Have you ever noticed that the older a man gets, the more athletic he was in his youth?

We get especially nostalgic when remembering our childhood. I remember long summer days on a farm with my brother and two cousins. On a piece of land not fit to grow anything but brambles, nature had carved out a big hole in the gentle side of a sloping grassy plain. The hole, about eight feet across, looked like a giant cereal bowl sitting in the backside of the pasture. We four cousins dragged fallen branches over the top of the hole to form a ceiling for our summer cave. We played in the cave for hours and hours, emerging only to fill our water jugs or negotiate another bag of cookies.

But I don't as often recall a life without central heat. One at a time, we children would pull on our pajamas in front of the fire and then make a mad dash for the bedcovers in the back room, which was closed off from the fireplace's warmth. Nor do I remember the bouts of flu. Nor the bad colds and runny noses. Nor the tonsillitis. Nor all the other illnesses brought on by cold weather. No, shivering under the bedclothes those cold nights doesn't come to mind as often as the big cave in the grassy pasture.

We generally remember the long-ago times as better than they really were.

Memory glitches also occur with jobs and careers. Someone may recall with pride and fondness the good old days when she worked at Sack-and-Save as a cashier. What good times she had with her friends at work. The good-looking guys. The Friday afternoon pizza parties. She forgets that while she held that job, she disliked the supervisor, the hours, the products, and the customers.

As a salesperson on the route, a fellow might aspire to being the national sales manager with a nice office, a big salary, and privileges at the country club. Then twenty years later, when he has reached his goal, he longs for the good old days, with nothing to worry about but assigned accounts and predictable hours.

Someone else might remember what a good friend Suzanne was—how she used to lend her skis and down jacket. She forgets that Suzanne also borrowed her tennis racket and broke it to smithereens without any offer to replace it.

It's a common malady. With friends, with jobs, with family, with childhood—time alters our memories and changes our perspective.

That's something to take into consideration on a rainy Sunday afternoon. The good we remember as better. The bad we remember as worse. The TV jingles we remember word for word.

But where memory is concerned, accuracy should not always be the goal. Remembering troubling times, complex circumstances, and wrong words can separate us from loved ones forever. Those memories can rust relationships.

We remember the family holiday when one sister-in-law commented to another sister-in-law about the overdone turkey. We forget to send a thank-you note for the hand-embroidered scarf.

We remember the broken chair for which someone failed to apologize. We remember the cousin's kids who ransacked the house for lack of supervision.

We forget to let our friends know our exact moving day.

Then they don't call to say good-bye, and we cross them off our list forever.

We remember a father's comment about our "rebellious teenage years," when the years themselves have already become a blur.

Memories are both accurate and inaccurate at the wrong times. Memories can ruin relationships. And we are worse for the missed connections with family and friends through the years. If asked, God will dim our memories of the unpleasant and refresh our memories of the good.

"Whatever is true, whatever is noble, whatever is right, whatever is pure, whatever is lovely, whatever is admirable—if anything is excellent or praiseworthy—think about such things" (Philippians 4:8).

■ ■ ■

Old men's eyes are like old men's memories; they are strongest for things a long way off.

—GEORGE ELIOT

Poor memory has its benefits. Otherwise a person would remember the times he has been a fool.

—UNKNOWN

Whenever I dwell for any length of time on my own shortcomings, they gradually begin to seem mild, harmless, rather engaging little things, not at all like the glaring ones in other people's characters.

—MARGARET HALSEY

Something Special Just for You

Shortly after my grandson's second birthday, we quickly determined that every little boy should have a rocking horse. How could we have waited so long? So with fervor, we began to shop for just the right horse. It had to be safe—well balanced on the platform, with a bridle just the right length so it couldn't get looped around our grandson's neck. The horse had to be big enough to last until he was bored with rocking horses. It had to be small enough for him to climb astride without help. It had to rock smoothly and easily; we didn't want him to have to work too hard to gallop. It had to be silent—none of those squeaky springs that set nerves on edge. It had to be colorful and bright, in keeping with the décor of his room.

So we shopped. And shopped. Mall after mall. Catalog after catalog. Finally, we found the perfect horse, brought it home, and hid it in its stable, the closet.

At the appointed hour, we turned on the Christmas tree lights, got the cameras set to flash, placed the horse under the tree, and called Mason into the room, expecting him to squeal with delight as soon as he laid eyes on that stallion.

"Mason, look. See what special things are under the tree for you!" We watched with happy hearts, wide eyes, and opened mouths.

Mason came. Mason saw. Mason walked away. The empty boxes proved to be far more fun than the toy we had so carefully chosen.

To date, the rocking horse has been ridden fewer than three times. My husband and I have since laughed at the choice. We realized we'd bought Mason what my husband had enjoyed as a child without considering that Mason had never expressed any interest in a rocking horse at all.

Along with the insight and laughter, we must admit that it was a disappointment to see a gift so lovingly chosen discarded with so little thought. One Saturday evening, after tucking Mason in and returning the horse to the closet, again unridden, I got a glimpse of how God must often feel. How many perfect gifts has he given to us—spouse, family, job, health, home, friends, nature, life—only to have them ignored or even rejected without recognition or gratitude?

■ ■ ■

Every good and perfect gift is from above, coming down from the Father of the heavenly lights.

—JAMES 1:17

What do you have that you did not receive?

—1 CORINTHIANS 4:7

Gratitude is the heart's memory.

—FRENCH PROVERB

When you drink the water, remember the spring.

—CHINESE PROVERB

I Think We Must
Have a Bad Connection

We were hoping to hire an administrative assistant who had the same exuberance as the one leaving the job. At least, that was the game plan as we began the search. As I sorted through the file of résumés we'd collected, I dreaded the thought of hours and even days of interviewing to find just the right person. When clients and prospects call our office, the first voice they hear makes a lasting impression. If that initial call is handled well, a prospect may become a client for life. If not, a caller may never give us a second chance.

That's why I get personally involved in hiring our front-line people. If our own employees can't demonstrate excellent communication skills on the phone, how can we convince clients that we can teach those skills in our training classes? That's my motivation for finding a receptionist who connects with people by demonstrating genuine warmth rather than one who considers the ringing phone an interruption.

So with that mind-set, I answered my phone and talked to Marilyn, whose name sounded vaguely familiar. She reintroduced herself and reminded me that I'd interviewed her by phone about four weeks earlier for the administrative assistant job.

"Yes, I do remember your earlier call," I told her. "But didn't you tell me then that you had just accepted a job offer the day after mailing your résumé to us?"

"Yes, I did." She paused slightly, then continued, "But that job turned out to be very short-lived. I worked there only about two weeks before they decided to do away with that department. So I'm job-hunting again and decided to call you back to let you know that I'm available if the position is still open."

I confirmed that it was. She continued to tell me about her skills and her previous work experience while I tried to read my scribbled notes from the earlier interview. My mind roamed between delight and reservation. I began to think aloud to her, "That's really strange, isn't it? Hiring you and then doing away with your job after just two weeks?"

"Yes, it is," she agreed. "But you know the way large corporations operate. Sometimes the left hand doesn't know what the right hand's doing."

She had a point. Mergers, acquisitions, and divestitures have been part of the corporate landscape for so long that her conclusion seemed likely. I set up an appointment for her to come in and asked for the name and number of her most recent supervisor. A two-week reference was better than no reference at all.

I hung up the phone puzzled at my own lack of enthusiasm. After all, we needed to fill the position quickly, and she looked good on paper. Although I couldn't put my finger on anything specific, there was something in her voice that troubled me. Her diction was impeccable. Her etiquette was proper. Her experience seemed impressive. Her age and life style indicated stability. The only negative was a distance in her tone and manner. Was it over-efficiency? Simply her New York accent and assertiveness? Defensiveness? Aloofness? Sadness? I could hear it, but I couldn't name it.

So I dialed the number of her previous supervisor. I explained the situation to him, repeated the applicant's explanation about why her recent job had lasted only two weeks, and asked for confirmation of the facts.

He hesitated a moment and then said, "Well, let me put it this way. We laid off a department, yes, but her job was the only job in that department."

I understood his between-the-lines message and probed further. "Was she efficient?"

"Yes, very efficient."

"Does she have the computer skills that she claims on her résumé?"

"Yes, she was excellent on the computer. She did several proposals for us, with all the whiz-bang graphics."

"How about writing skills—did she handle your correspondence?"

"Yes, we had her do letters for several of the engineers. No complaints there."

"Was she honest? On time? Productive?"

"OK on all those." After a slight pause, he added, "Yeah, she kept busy all right."

"Yet you let her go after two weeks?"

"She just didn't work out." He hesitated again, offering the same meaningless answer that didn't fill in the gaps.

Finally I said, "Look, I know people are hesitant to give references for fear of lawsuits, but we're a small business, and we can't afford to make a mistake with an employee. Our employees routinely interact with our clients, and this position is an important one. I really would appreciate any insights at all that you could give us. She looks very good on paper. I, . . . well, I just had a slight hesitation about her manner on the phone."

Finally I sparked a response. He said, "Ah, you noticed it, too."

"Well, I noticed something, but I couldn't quite label it. I chalked it up to her sounding hurt and disappointed that her job didn't work out."

"Now that you've brought it up, I will tell you this: It was not exactly what she said—it was what she didn't say. In her two-week tenure here, three clients commented on her manner on the phone. One of them said something like, 'She sounds awfully busy.' Another one commented that he thought he'd somehow made her angry. And another client said, 'She doesn't have a lot of fun, does she?' You get the idea—she just wouldn't or couldn't connect with people, you know what I mean?"

I did. And I thanked him. We didn't proceed with the interview. My earlier gut reaction had been too strong to deny, and his comments confirmed my reservations.

Years have passed. I have interviewed hundreds of applicants during the past twenty years in business. I've interviewed some people who lied on their résumés. Some were emotionally troubled. Some lacked skills or experience. Some held unrealistic expectations about salaries and opportunities. Some lacked initiative and motivation. But I remember my two phone conversations with Marilyn for no other reason than her coldness.

Whether from disappointments in childhood, the loneliness of broken relationships, or bitterness about a lack of education or employment opportunity, many people go through life surrounded by an invisible wall. Initially they may have erected the wall as a way of protecting themselves, but over time it turned into a wall of rejection. Protection from the pain of change. Rejection of those who might ask them to try.

Yes, letting others inside our lives and hearts may open us to pain, pressure, and pursuit. But along with that risk, others may also offer understanding, acceptance, and love. To feel a connection with others, sometimes all that's necessary is to improve our own reception.

▪ ▪ ▪

Some people are molded by their admiration, others by their hostility.

—ELIZABETH BOWEN

It's funny how your initial approach to a person can determine your feelings toward them, no matter what facts develop later on.

—DOROTHY UHNAK

Ideal conversation must be an exchange of thought, and not, as many of those who worry most about their shortcomings believe, an eloquent exhibition of wit or oratory.

—EMILY POST

What Do You Think?
I Made It Myself

When I got off the train in the little burg in upstate New York, I began to think the publicist had made some kind of mistake. Had I looked at the wrong date in my day planner and then gotten on the wrong plane, awakened in the wrong city, and then taken the wrong train? Surely, this out-of-the-way place couldn't be the home of an important cable TV show. I'd just come from a whirlwind of interviews in New York City and Los Angeles; the contrast couldn't have been more startling.

Someone called my name, and I turned around to see a tiny older woman holding a copy of my book *Ten Smart Moves for Women*. She stuck out her hand and introduced herself as the host of the show. Another omen. The host of the show rarely shows up in the studio more than ninety seconds before airtime. I had expected, at best, the assistant producer to meet me at the train station. I followed her to her car.

She talked nonstop about famous guests she had hosted in years past—some thirty years past. She talked from the moment she laid eyes on me until we pulled into a treelined street in a residential neighborhood. When I looked quizzically at the unexpected destination, she said, "We're stopping by my house to pick up my husband. He's going to drive us on to the studio because he needs to use the car."

"Fine," I said. But as I glanced at my watch, my heart sank. The four o'clock train to Manhattan left in two hours, and I intended to be on it. If not, I would not be back in Dallas until the wee hours of the following morning. After a long week on the road, another night on an airplane didn't sound enticing.

The car horn sounded, and a white-haired man in a gray sweater shuffled out to the car and slid behind the wheel. My TV host introduced me to Henry, her husband of fifty-two years. Then we were off again, roaring along at about twenty miles per hour. Now both of them continued the travel-guide commentary as we passed the post office, the grocery store, the elementary school, and whatever else lay between us and the interview. It was not that I had anything against learning about upstate New York; it was only that I had to make that four o'clock train back to Manhattan.

Live shows happen on time. All guests and crew live or die, speak or shut up, by the studio clock. But when taping for later broadcast, things often lag behind schedule. I knew we were scheduled for a fifty-minute interview. Not much dawdle time built in. Almost as if reading my mind, she turned around to the backseat to ask, "Are you planning to make the four o'clock train back to the city?"

"Yes, I am," I said, glad for the opportunity to confirm that we were on the same wavelength about the afternoon schedule.

"There is another train at six o'clock, you know. I thought you might like to take your time so we didn't have to rush after your interview."

"Well, I'd love to take my time, but if I don't make the four o'clock train, I won't make my flight out of La Guardia, and that means I won't be home until about three in the morning."

"I see."

I got the distinct feeling that she didn't.

It seemed we were taking a circuitous route back toward the train station where she'd just picked me up, and I was becoming a little perturbed. Yes, it was a lovely fall afternoon, and the red, gold, and purple leaves lay in beautiful piles everywhere I looked. If I had been on a leisurely vacation, I could have appreciated the scenery. But I had a show to do and a husband to get home to.

When Henry finally announced, "Well, I'll be back for you girls shortly," and turned off the highway to let us out, I did a double take. The recording studio was not exactly CNN Center. As soon as we ascended the front stairs, my host introduced me to the makeup artist/hair stylist who would come get me "after a while" and excused herself to touch up her makeup. After she had disappeared, I pulled out my calendar and notes.

Surely there was some mistake. I must have misunderstood how important my publisher had said this interview would be to the book's promotion to the literary elite of New York. I reread the notes. No, that's what Jane had said. My interviewer was a well-respected literary figure with a large audience.

OK. Just do it, I said to myself. Watch the clock, cut the chitchat every chance you get. The four o'clock train is a must.

"I like to do a little preinterview, if you don't mind," she said, pulling out what appeared to be about fifteen pages of notes along with my book.

"That would be great," I said sincerely. "It's so infrequent that an interviewer has even read the book, much less prepared notes!"

"Is that right?" she beamed. "Well, I do prepare. Well."

Half an hour later, I understood the extent of her preparation. She had almost written herself a script, including all the key questions and transitions between them. She pronounced me "ready to go on the air."

The guest being taped before me was "taking longer than expected," I soon learned. As we waited, my host pulled out her guest books to entertain me. As she turned the pages to show me photographs of the literary legends she'd personally interviewed, I was indeed impressed.

Her face glowed as she recounted her interview with each one. A scrap about a book here, a memorable quote from an interview there. "Elegant," she said often about some of the authors and movie stars of the 1950s and 1960s. "They were elegant—left just enough to the imagination to be sexy and glamorous. Not the Madonna image at all. These women were classy."

I became truly fascinated as she shared the photos and her reminiscences with me. She was delightful and witty. And her pleasure in showing me her keepsakes was obvious.

But time was still the issue.

"I'm not sure you're going to make your four o'clock train," she said when she noticed me glance at my watch again. "Are you sure you wouldn't rather take the six or the eight o'clock? My husband is an artist, you know. We thought you might have time to stop by our home to see his sculpture."

"That sounds really enjoyable. But I really need to make that four o'clock train if I'm going to get home tonight. I've been on the road all week."

She nodded but her expression betrayed a twinge of disappointment.

Finally we were called into the studio, and the interview was underway. She was the perfect host, asking exactly the questions she had said she would. As soon as they called it a wrap, I glanced at my watch. There was still time to make the four o'clock train. Barely.

"Just have a seat up front," she said to me. "I'll put my things back in my office, and we'll wait for my husband."

I stood. Through the windows, I watched the breeze gently swirling the golden leaves up and around. It was truly a day made in heaven. If only . . . she joined me just as her husband pulled into the parking lot. As we started down the steps toward the car, she said, "Henry's going to be so disappointed. He just loves for people to see his sculpture."

"I'd love to have time to do that. But I'm afraid to take a chance on missing that four o'clock train."

She looked at her watch. "I think we could spend maybe fifteen minutes at the house anyway before taking you back to the train."

It really wasn't a question. So I said, "Well, I don't know exactly where we are and how long it'll take us to drive back to the train. I'll have to trust your judgment on that."

She beamed. We climbed back into the car. "Henry, Dianna wants to see your sculpture. So let's go back by there on the way to the train."

"Wonderful, wonderful," he said. "We love having company; we sure do."

They continued the tour-guide explanations as we passed through various neighborhoods. Within five minutes we pulled up in their yard again and went inside the small brick home.

The house had become a museum. A piece of sculpture occupied every available inch on every end table, dining table, kitchen table, game table, bookshelf, desk, and credenza. More than four hundred pieces altogether. Each piece was made from something you might find at Home Depot—hammers, nails, screws, scraps of tin, levels, pulleys, wrenches, wires. Each sculpture was labeled and priced— most around $2,000, although a few peaked at $12,000.

He took one arm and she took the other as we began the tour. Each piece had its own unique flow, essence, statement. He explained each piece; she complimented his work. He beamed. She responded with a "you're welcome" smile.

Henry mumbled something about photos and shuffled into another room for a moment.

"Well, I guess we need to leave now if you want to make the four o'clock train. But we sure wish you could stay awhile longer," she paused to catch my eye. "There's a six o'clock train, you know. Henry's going to be so disappointed. You didn't even get to see the pieces in the breakfast room and the bedroom. Is this boring, or are you enjoying this?"

"No, no," I said sincerely. "It's wonderful. These are truly ingenious creations. I just wish I wasn't so tired and hadn't been traveling so many days."

Henry returned bearing photos of his art shows and a camera. "Let me take a picture of you two girls before we go."

We posed. He snapped.

"I could get you some lemonade," she said. "Lemonade would be really refreshing. Henry, tell her about that piece over there while I get us some lemonade. She said she could take the six o'clock train."

Henry shuffled to the doorway of the next room. "Are you sure?"

he asked, without waiting for my answer. "We'll have no problem making the six o'clock train—you'll be fine. You'll get to see the Iris Dive piece. Almost sold that for $12,000. May still yet. Now, take a look at this piece here. Let me tell you what all went into this creation. First, I had to find these certain railroad spikes—and those are hard to come by nowadays."

I accepted the glass of lemonade and followed him to the next piece. Some things are more meaningful than making flight connections. If only we recognize them.

■ ■ ■

The best index to a person's character is (a) how he treats people who can't do him any good, and (b) how he treats people who can't fight back.

—ABIGAIL VAN BUREN

We are rich only through what we give, and poor only through what we refuse.

—ANNE-SOPHIE SWETCHINE

Unfortunately, sometimes people don't hear you until you scream.

—STEPHANIE POWERS

Night Talk

Do you remember the country-and-western song by Charlie Rich called "Behind Closed Doors"? The refrain goes something like this: "When the sun goes down and my baby lets her hair hang down, no one knows what goes on behind closed doors."

Do you think the songwriter is talking about chitchat? Neither do I, but he could have been. That's when most people do their most serious talking. Have you ever heard anyone say he's going home at lunchtime to discuss a pending divorce? Or have you ever discovered two college coeds sharing secrets at four in the afternoon? There's just something about the nighttime that invites intimacy of the soul.

At the age of twelve during a sleep-over, my best friend and I promised to be in each other's weddings. A retired army general sitting beside me on a late evening flight reflected on the pleasures of his colorful past in stations all over the world but then grew serious as he shared his regrets about missing important family events and his feelings of failure as a father. Over a late-night dinner, a friend solemnly explained to me why she'd stayed with an abusive husband for twenty-five years.

Women seem to find night talk easier than men do. We start with those slumber-party conversations about boys who've jilted us, feeling overweight, our crush on the P.E. teacher, and our parents' selfishness in getting divorced before we finish junior high. As women, we graduate to subjects such as our insensitive and unromantic husbands, the effects of a job change on our long-term career plans, mother-induced guilt, and our confusion when our children rebel.

But such nighttime intimacy is not entirely foreign to men. In a late-night ride across country, a salesman shares with his boss his conviction that God used the death of his child to punish him. A college-age son throws himself across the end of his dad's bed at midnight to ask if his current girlfriend is wife material. In foxholes under the cover of dark, soldiers share their fears and philosophies about dying.

Nighttime is the time for intimate conversation. These are intimacies we would never share in daylight—at least not with the same people at the same level of honesty. In the morning light after such a soul baring, we may blush to think of what we've shared. What's more confusing, we may no longer even believe it. Our hope or sense of helplessness often rises and sets with the sun.

What is it about darkness that overcomes our defenses and inhibitions and connects us on a deeper dimension? God is the invisible and often unacknowledged connection to others in ways that we can't explain, even to ourselves. We confess sins. We ask for forgiveness. We express fears. We seek advice. We challenge authority. We share love. We reminisce about roots. We reevaluate our past. We plan our future.

God made both the day and the night, and He said both are good. Darkness often illuminates the soul and frees the tongue. In the still dark of the hospital room, at the dimly lit graveside, in the darkness of our own bewilderment, we can count on Him to sit up with us. We can take great comfort that God never sleeps—so we can.

■ ■ ■

My help comes from the LORD, the Maker of heaven and earth. He will not let your foot slip—he who watches over you will not slumber . . . The sun will not harm you by day, nor the moon by night. The LORD will keep you from all harm—he will watch over your life.

—PSALM 121:2–3, 6–7

To be rooted is perhaps the most important and least recognized need of the human soul.

—SIMONE WEIL

Prayer is more than meditation. In meditation the source of strength is one's self. When one prays he goes to a source of strength greater than his own.

—MADAME CHIANG KAI-SHEK

Love in Your Luggage

A few years ago, I left West Palm Beach, Florida, for Minneapolis, where I had a workshop the next morning at eight o'clock. My itinerary showed a one-hour stopover in Atlanta. After sitting on the runway most of that hour, we arrived at the gate three minutes before my next flight's departure time. I was sitting in the second row in coach. If I could just get around the guy in front of me, who stood between me and the door . . .

He planted his feet firmly in the center of the aisle. "Just hold your horses," he said as he hiked up his pants and reached into the overhead compartment for his bags and hat. "If I missed my flight, you're gonna miss yours." Helplessly, I watched him slowly dig through his bags, methodically repack them, crawl into his coat, and then saunter off the plane. One minute until flight time.

The attendant, with clipboard in hand, met us at the end of the ramp. I yelled, "Which gate to Minneapolis?"

"You're in luck—right in front of you. They've still got the door open." He pointed to the gate directly across from where I stood.

I waved at the gate agent. "Wait. I'm coming." She took my ticket and closed the door behind me.

Relieved and breathing heavily, I dragged my two bags to the back row, shoved them in the overhead compartment, and fell into the seat. Just as we began to back away from the gate, the flight attendant began the announcements. She finished by saying, "So thank you for flying with us this evening. We will be landing in Charlotte in about one hour."

Charlotte? Charlotte, North Carolina? I grabbed another attendant as she moved down the aisle. "Where's this plane going?" She looked at me as if she were hearing-impaired. "I've got to get off. Your gate agent told me this plane was going to Minneapolis."

A moment later, the same voice droned over the P.A., "I'm sorry, ladies and gentlemen, we're going to have to taxi back to the gate. We have a passenger on the wrong plane."

I tried not to look at anyone as I fumbled my bags back down the aisle and off the plane. The gate attendant still stood outside the boarding ramp, counting her tickets.

"Which gate to Minneapolis? They put me on the wrong flight. I need my ticket back."

"Ma'am, you really have to assume some of the responsibility to listen to boarding announcements."

"Listen to announcements? Your agent—"

"We announced the destination of this plane three times while passengers were seated here in the boarding area."

"But I wasn't seated here in your boarding area. I was sitting on the runway on your late plane. And your agent told me—never mind, just give me my ticket. They're closing the next gate. I'm going to miss that one, too."

"Just wait. You'll have to wait until I locate your ticket." She continued to mumble under her breath. "The entire plane had to come back because of this—you really should—"

"Just give me my ticket." I grabbed it and ran. Just as I got to the next gate, the surly agent closed it.

"I'm sorry, you're too late." Her expression did not convey regret.

"But your agent told me—"

"The plane has taken off."

Finally, I located a plane going to Minneapolis at 11:30. I waited the three hours. There was a rainstorm. We left at 1:30 A.M., and I arrived at my hotel about 4:30 A.M. only to hear the desk clerk say, "We've given your room away. We had no idea you planned to arrive so late."

I finally talked the clerk into giving me a room under construction with a rollaway bed for the sixty minutes remaining before my morning workshop was to begin. No sooner had I unpacked my bag than there was a knock at the door.

The bell captain handed me a package. Inside the large suit-size Federal Express box, there was a note. It read: "I listened to the weather report for West Palm and then for Minneapolis. Thought you might need your coat. I love you."

Upon reflection, I've discovered that many people's daily lives are like some of those travel schedules: a series of missed connections with jobs, frustrations with family, and disappointments with duty—too early for this and too late for that.

In our technologically wired world, the more easily we can connect with others, the less connected we feel. Relationships with those around us make the difference between disease and health, depression and happiness, despair and hope. Encourage each other with reminders. Love holds us together when everything else falls apart.

■ ■ ■

Time is . . .
Too slow for those who wait,
Too swift for those who fear,
Too long for those who rejoice.
But for those who love,
Time is not.

—HENRY VAN DYKE, *For Katrina's Sun-Dial*

And now these three remain: faith, hope and love. But the greatest of these is love.

—1 CORINTHIANS 13:13

The healthy and strong individual is the one who asks for help when he needs it. Whether he's got an abscess on his knee or in his soul.

—RONA BARRETT

I Wait Six Hours and Take More?

Promptly at 10:30 P.M., my husband and I pulled up to the curb at the airport terminal and waited in the taxi zone. In a couple of moments, Hilaire, in his spiffy new security guard uniform, walked out of the terminal, glancing from car to car. He looked like a young child lost in a maze of adults in a crowded mall. My husband lowered our tinted window on the passenger side, and a smile of recognition flashed across Hilaire's face. He opened the back door and crawled inside.

For several weeks he had depended on others to take him to his job and return him to his apartment each night. On this particular night, he had little to say as he quietly settled in.

As my husband pulled out into traffic, he asked, "How do you feel tonight?"

Hilaire pulled at his throat. "Still no good." He shook his head, coughed, and put the back of his hand toward his forehead as a mother would check a child for fever. "Hot. No . . . good," he said in broken English.

My husband had taken a late lunch hour and had driven Hilaire to work earlier that afternoon. He'd mentioned to me that Hilaire seemed to be fighting either a cold or his first case of the flu in the United States.

His English was getting better every day, and we complimented him on it.

He smiled broadly. "I can practice every day now. I read grammar book you give every morning. Two hours, I read. Very simple. Good to understand. Thank you very much."

Like most refugees in the United States, Hilaire came with a history. He simply showed up one Sunday morning at our church, along with another man from the Congo. And the next week and the next week and the next. Because of the language barrier, it had been difficult to get past the ritualistic greeting, welcome, and handshake. But both the church group and Hilaire persisted. Curiosity and generosity intertwined to ferret out his story.

He had come to the United States to attend a conference sponsored by an evangelistic organization. While he was here, civil war had broken out in his country and officials there closed the only airport. He could not return to his wife and family, nor could they leave the country to come to him, even if they had had the money.

Formerly a professor of French at a Congolese university, Hilaire set about trying to make sense of this unexpected turn of events. His first obstacle was registering for a green card so that he could stay in the U.S. legally. Having accomplished that feat, he began to look for a job so that he could save enough money to bring his family to this country. Although his wife had a job in the Congo, her life alone with their two children in the war-torn country was growing more unpredictable by the moment.

During recent weeks, Hilaire had phoned her and learned that she had not received her last two paychecks. The government had taken control of the telephone systems and closed down the postal system. He could no longer write to her, and his phone calls were connected only through the goodwill of a friend, who visited his wife at appointed times and took his cellular phone to her. When Hilaire's call came through, the friend would hand the phone to Hilaire's wife and hold the baby while they talked twelve or twenty-four minutes, depending on how many minutes were left on Hilaire's prepaid phone card. Part of the "conversation" included listening to his new baby cry, a welcome sound because this second child had been born while Hilaire was in the United States.

As we pulled onto the freeway leaving the airport, my husband asked him, "When do you think your friend will get the car repaired?"

"I hope soon," Hilaire said, pronouncing each word separately and crisply. "I give him the $400 last week. But he say he has not time to buy parts. He need money for groceries. He buy parts maybe next week and fix car."

My husband filled me in on this exchange. A taxi driver, also originally from the Congo but living in the United States for the past twelve years, had attended the same conference that had brought Hilaire to this country. When Hilaire learned he could not go home, the taxi driver had invited him to stay in his two-bedroom apartment—along with his pregnant wife and two teenagers. Hilaire had been paying him $250 a month to live with them. The taxi driver had told Hilaire that he could drive his older, second car to work—if he could find a job. Having gotten the job as a security guard at the airport, checking luggage as it moved through x-ray machines, Hilaire had taken the clunker to work and had a fender bender in it. The taxi-driver friend told him that he must pay $400 to get it repaired. Our Bible-study group had put together a sign-up list for those who could drive him to work at 2:00 P.M. and pick him up at 10:30 P.M. each day during this period without a car.

"I've found a mechanic who says he'll repair the car with no charge to you," my husband said. "He owns his own shop and goes to our church. They can pick up the car, install the parts, and bring it back to you. Did you tell your friend that?"

"I tell my friend," Hilaire said. "I tell him, but he says he no want the free mechanic. He want to take it to his own friend to repair. He spend the $400 I give him on groceries. He will buy the parts and fix the car maybe next week when he get more money."

From an outsider's perspective, it was difficult to tell from the last exchange whether the taxi-driver friend was helping Hilaire or Hilaire's money was helping the taxi-driver friend.

"Have you been able to save much money?" my husband asked.

"They pay me $6.50 every hour. I save $600. I pay $400 to my friend to repair car. I have $200 left. Susan put it in her bank for me."

He referred to the woman in our Bible-study group who had graciously organized the effort to drive him back and forth to his job during these weeks without the car.

"How much will it cost to bring your family here?" I asked him.

"Maybe $6,000. The man checked airline for me. I maybe get raise. Save more. Long time."

Then Hilaire brought up the grammar book again, telling me how much it was helping him learn the language. He had already noted how similar English is to other Romance languages, particularly French, which he spoke fluently.

"I hope to teach at university when I learn more better English. I talked to the university last week. I gave them," he groped for the word *application*, which we offered, and he continued, "application and asked if I teach French. They say I must speak English more better first. When I learn English good, I come back to ask job again."

I nodded. Except for one long year overseas, I've always been surrounded by family or friends, have spoken the native tongue, and have had money in my pocketbook. It was difficult to fathom his predicament. Yet he remained optimistic.

Except for this evening. The sparkle in his eyes was not quite as bright, and his tone was not quite as cheerful.

"Would you like us to stop and get some medicine?" I said when he coughed again.

"OK," he said simply, and we lapsed again into silence. From his tone, I could tell he didn't know whether I had asked him a question or made a statement. Maybe he didn't understand the word medicine.

When my husband pulled off the freeway and into the deserted Kroger's parking lot after 11:00 P.M., it occurred to me that he couldn't buy himself medicine because he couldn't read the labels. So we began another sign-language exchange to verify his symptoms. The two men waited in the car while I went inside and stocked up on various cold remedies.

When I returned to the car with the bag of goodies, I felt like a mother talking to the baby-sitter about the newborn she was about to leave for the first time. First I pulled out the cough syrup, hacked a few times myself so he'd know the symptom he was trying to alleviate, and then pulled the plastic cup off the bottle to show him the amount to swallow.

"I wait six hour and take more?"

"Yes. Six hours. Take more. Six hours. Take more."

We repeated the procedure for the Tylenol, the Contac, and the throat lozenges. After I'd acted out the symptoms and had gone through the dosages, the time of day, and the frequency, he said, "OK, I say back to you." Then he proceeded to repeat everything to verify that he had correctly linked the cough to the cough syrup and the fever to the Tylenol.

As we pulled into the apartment complex, he smiled and said simply, "Thank you very much. Good night." He got out and disappeared into the dark stairwell leading to his friend's second-story apartment.

As I stared into the darkness after him, I saw his very life ebb and flow on trust. Trust in his taxi-driver friend with the car and the apartment. Trust in Susan and her bank account. Trust in his employer to pay him accurately. Trust in the medication that we had decided he should take. Trust in the system that a strange country had laid out before him. Trust in his God who promised, "I am with you always."

Those who trust us build in us accountability and honor. We come to know ourselves through their dependence.

■ ■ ■

Those who trust us educate us.

—George Eliot

Whoever trusts in the LORD is kept safe.

—Proverbs 29:25

Whose Fault Is This Mess?

Moving day. Just thinking about it has been known to bring on nervous tremors. There are so many things that can go wrong that the law of averages says something will. So with the best-laid-plans philosophy in mind, we began to schedule our business move across town into a new bank building.

My husband and our office manager had covered all the bases with the moving company, the phone company, the utility companies, the building manager, the office-furniture installers, and the computer consultants. We had employees with emergency files and stand-alone computers staked out in both the old location and the new to cover any client calls on the day of the big phone switch-over.

What we didn't plan on was things going awry from the first hour.

The moving van had loaded us up after the close of business on Thursday and pulled into the bank parking lot at ten o'clock the next morning to begin unloading. The office-furniture installers were to arrive two hours earlier, at eight o'clock, to set up the new modular furniture that was to occupy the main area of our new offices.

The furniture-installation crew held the keys to the kingdom.

Their furniture had to be in place before the phone and computer cables could be strung through the area. We needed the phone and computer cables in place before we could unload the equipment onto the desks. Our employees couldn't be fully functional until phones and computers were functioning at each desk.

So you can see why we greeted the furniture installers with a grand welcome when they arrived promptly at the scheduled time. As the installers scurried around, carrying in and opening up boxes of partitions and desk tops, I began to relax. Maybe this was going to happen like clockwork. Congratulations were in order for my husband and our office manager for pulling the whole effort together.

But standing inside my own still-empty office, I could see the three installers huddled in conversation. It was their quiet whispers that got my attention. I walked into the open space.

The supervisor of the crew was just beginning to explain the problem to the office manager: "It doesn't fit together."

"What do you mean, it doesn't fit together?" I asked. "I thought all this modular stuff was supposed to be interchangeable?"

"Well, not exactly. Looks like these panels aren't the right size to fit those panels."

"Well, can't you go ahead and install all the rest of this stuff so we can begin to run the phone and computer cables?"

About this time, the phone installation crew arrived, along with the computer consultants. Right on time. Nine o'clock.

"Nope," the furniture installer said. "The panels that don't fit are the main ones that hold the rest of the desk surfaces and walls together."

I let out a sigh of exasperation. At just that moment, Tom, the account rep who had sold us the furniture, walked in. He joined the huddle and shook hands all around. "So how's it going here?"

We told him.

He swallowed hard. "Let me get on the phone and take care of it."

Take care of it? *That sounds promising*, I muttered to myself. So there was probably a quick solution after all. He'd call the warehouse and have someone scramble over with replacement partitions.

Tom disappeared into a vacant office, away from the hubbub, to make his phone call. The telephone crew and the computer crew shuffled and harrumphed about not being able to begin their parts of this moving relay. We hemmed and hawed, stalling until Tom got off the phone.

The moving-van crew continued to lug in piece after piece and box after box and set them down all around us. Since no cubicles were standing, the site map we'd hung on the walls to show them exactly where the neatly color-coded boxes and furniture should go were of absolutely no use. Instead, they piled the boxes wherever the notion struck them. We began to envision the hours of time, not to mention the strong backs, it would require to move all the items once again after the modular furniture was in place.

Tom finally hung up the phone and reappeared from the empty office. His expression was grim. "Looks like we have the wrong pieces."

Raised eyebrows and smirks all around. We knew that.

He continued, "I wish I could blame the manufacturer for sending the wrong panels. Or the customer-service people. That's why I took so long on the phone. I had my assistant pull all the paperwork and double-check our original order. But," he hesitated a moment, shaking his head, "it looks like the mistake was mine. I just wrote down the wrong catalog numbers. It's all my fault."

He paused then added, "And we don't have anything in the Dallas warehouse that will work. We're going to have to replace the order with the manufacturer and wait until they can ship new panels. That'll take at least two weeks. We can't finish your installation for at least two weeks. I have no one to blame but myself, and I know this is a terrible imposition, to say the least. I'm sorry."

One by one, the various groups began to grumble, pack up their tools, and mumble about rescheduling. One mistake caused our day's plans to fall like dominoes. Tom's announcement meant that on Monday morning, all our employees would report to work—with no work surfaces, no computer hookups, and no phones, except for those we could plug into wall jacks and set on the floor in various nooks and crannies.

Our office manager followed me into my empty office with the same question that was on my own mind: "Do we want to go to another company to reorder the furniture and handle the installation—or stay with Tom?"

I thought it over. I had grown all too accustomed to people passing the buck—or even lying—when things went wrong. Several typical conversations floated from the recesses of my mind:

"How was I supposed to know what to do with these packages?"

"The client is the one that didn't follow through—not me!"

"With all the stuff I've got on my plate, something was bound to go wrong. I'm only human, you know."

"That's not my job—I didn't know you were counting on me to think about that."

"That's out of my hands."

"They should have told me."

It occurred to me that Tom could easily have blamed the error on the manufacturer, and we'd never have known the difference. Since he had owned up to this mess, I reasoned, then he was probably also telling us the truth about the quality of furniture, the competitive price, and the kind of service his company would offer after the sale.

It suddenly seemed refreshing to find someone so committed to the truth. What a discovery—someone assuming personal responsibility for errors despite the personal consequences and the potential of lost commissions.

"No," I finally answered the office manager. "I think we have a winner in Tom. Let's wait and let him reorder."

Truth proves to be a powerful foundation for relationships, whether they are professional or personal. Eight years and two moves later, we're still doing business with Tom's company.

■ ■ ■

It is very easy to forgive others their mistakes; it takes more grit and gumption to forgive them for having witnessed your own.

—JESSAMYN WEST

Do you approach things with the thought "How can I make this work?" rather than "What happens if I fail?"

—BARBARA POPE

We increase our ability, stability, and responsibility when we increase our accountability to God.

—UNKNOWN

He who conceals his sins does not prosper, but whoever confesses and renounces them finds mercy.

—PROVERBS 28:13

Down a Long Flight of Stairs

I awoke early. It was an important day. Our nine o'clock meeting at the client's headquarters in Memphis would be our first official act as strategic partners, the beginning of a long and profitable relationship for both companies.

As usual in a hotel room, I paused at the side of the bed to get my bearings. With the moonlight shining through a crack in the drapes, the room's layout came back to me in nanoseconds. Maneuvering in a strange, darkened room is simply a matter of remembering how many luggage racks or chair legs may catch a bare toe between bed and bath.

So as not to wake my husband, I stepped into the bathroom and closed the door behind me before reaching for the light. He could use at least ten more minutes' sleep. No light. I flipped the switch again. Another switch. A third switch. No light. The bulb had apparently burned out.

No problem, I decided. I cracked the door slightly to catch a little of the moonlight through the bedroom drapes. I'd go ahead and take a shower in the dark and then wake my husband and ask him to call the front desk about getting the light bulb changed.

About two minutes into the shower, the hot water turned cold. Very cold. I finished shampooing quickly and stepped out into a warm towel.

"No hot water and no lights—the electricity must be off," I called to my husband. "Would you please call the front desk to see when it'll be back on?"

Don't panic. I congratulated myself on having the good sense to rise extra early to allow ample time to get to the meeting. It would definitely not bode well to keep five busy executives waiting for us.

"Yes, we're having a problem this morning," someone at the front desk reported on the phone. "One of the generators is out. We're working on it, and you should have power again shortly."

We waited. Still no power. We dialed again. Busy line, couldn't get through. By this time, with drapes wide open, enough sun was streaming in for us to dress and repack our luggage. But what to do about the wet hair, with no electricity for the blow-dryer and curling iron? And the bathroom, situated so that it got none of the light from the bedroom window, was far too dark to apply makeup in. At my age, this can be a serious problem.

Not in a panic yet, we concluded there was still ample time to make our meeting. We'd simply take a taxi, arrive early for the meeting, and finish our grooming rituals in a lobby rest room on-site.

Our goal became to get to the lobby. A trip to the elevator confirmed our fears—it was not operating. OK, we decided, we'd simply call the front desk and ask that a bellman be sent to our room to pick up our luggage, projector equipment, and books—four heavy cases in all. Then we'd take the stairs. The switchboard was busy. We waited. Dialed again. Waited. Dialed again. Waited. Dialed again.

Twenty minutes later, the operator finally answered, "The switchboard is jammed with calls. I'll try to get a bellman up to you, but don't count on it. It could be an hour or more."

"Ma'am, we're on the twenty-sixth floor. And we really need a bellman."

"That's the best I can do."

We waited another ten minutes. Another attempt on the phone. The phone line was dead.

An hour until meeting time. We decided to head for the staircase alone. Arms loaded with luggage and equipment, we maneuvered our way past the defunct elevator. Upon entering the pitch-black stairwell, we soon discovered the rest of humanity—all in the stairwell. As we descended each flight, more and more people joined in the parade headed toward light and safety on the ground level.

The conversations drifted to us from people a flight below or a flight above. "So I was right in the middle of ordering room service, and I just hung up the phone. No way am I going to eat what I can't see."

"I know what you mean. Food isn't all that good here anyway."

"I've got three bags."

"I was lucky; my partner had already taken our luggage down earlier this morning and had it stored for the day."

"This happened to me once in Philly. They never did get the electricity back on while I was there—two days I stayed at that hotel without lights."

"Why didn't you move?"

"Couldn't get reservations anywhere else. Big convention in town. What else could I do?"

"This is kinda like the night I spent in San Francisco when they had the last quake."

"Oh, yeah? Bet that was scary."

"Nothing like the fire we had in a hotel in Las Vegas. Stood outside in twenty-degree weather for two hours in the middle of the night."

"You'd think they'd have backup generators."

"They do. Somebody said it's an internal wiring problem. The rest of the hotel has power—it's just our tower."

That news struck panic in me. Did that mean that when we stepped out of the stairwell at ground level, everybody else would be coifed and clean, wondering what had happened to the rest of us?

"My wife told me to pack light—glad I listened to her."

"I never travel with more than one bag—a light one at that."

"I got a trade show this morning. Have to carry all this extra stuff that I don't normally travel with."

"Oh, yeah, right. Here, let me give you a hand with one of those."

The two shadowy people in front of me stopped and did a bag trade. New voices joined a flight or two above us.

"Man, I gotta get on a diet. I can't believe I'm this winded after only a few flights."

"Me, too. I feel faint."

I wondered how they'd ever get a paramedic to him in the dark. Follow the voices?

"How much farther?"

"I think we're at about the fifth floor now."

"No, still nine. I just came in from nine."

"Are you OK?" someone asked the voice ahead of me.

"I've got to stop and rest."

"Yeah. Good idea. Rest. Take it easy, a couple of flights at a time."

"When I get down, I'm going to see if they can't send a bellman up the stairwell if the elevators are still not running."

"Thanks. I'll wait here."

What seemed like hours later, my husband and I emerged from the stairwell into the ground floor lobby. And to my chagrin, everyone who passed us in the lobby looked quite normal. I tried to duck my wet head as people's eyes glanced furtively from head to toe to take in the incongruent sight—business suit, high heels, briefcase, no make-up, wet hair.

At the front desk, the rumor proved true. "Sorry about the inconvenience," the desk clerk said. "But it only affected your tower. We had a generator problem that knocked out the lights, phones, and hot-water heaters. It should be restored sometime today. The rest of the building's fine." She beamed a broad smile at us, as if that was supposed to be good news.

"Is there an electrical outlet in the rest room in the lobby so I can do my hair?" I asked.

"I doubt it." She seemed most unconcerned. "There's a janitorial closet with a mirror on the back of the door over there. You might find an electrical outlet in there."

I did. Between the shelves of paper towels. Dodging the brooms, smelling disinfectant, and restacking the toilet paper to allow space for my curling iron, I settled into the makeshift dressing room. Within half an hour, I managed to apply makeup and dry and curl my hair. We arrived for our meeting on time.

Inconvenient, yes. Disaster, no.

What started out as a somber journey became lighter with each flight of stairs. How so? The camaraderie of the other people in the stairwell. They were showing concern and offering suggestions to people they might not have even spoken to in a concert audience. I had experienced the phenomenon so many times before. A hotel fire alarm at three o'clock in the morning. A grounded plane and an all-nighter at an airport. No signs or announcements in English in a foreign country. People feel a need to connect in times of puzzlement or misfortune.

By the time our meeting convened, the whole experience had become fodder for a good laugh.

In the taxi on the way to the airport the following day, my husband and I began to reflect on prior travel adventures and misadventures. We both had been struck by how cordial and even comical the conversations between dark shadows on the stairway had become. By the time our group from floors twenty-six to twenty-two emerged into the lobby after twenty minutes together in the stairwell, we felt as if we were saying so long to old friends.

I recalled the tornadoes that struck our small town of Bynum when I was a child. Seven of our neighbors were killed, and many more were injured that night. The rescuers used our house for their headquarters as they regrouped and left again to search for victims in the darkness.

At nineteen, I lived through a typhoon on Okinawa. The winds were so strong you could not walk from house to car. We cowered in our homes of concrete cinder blocks, windows covered with boards and bars to protect us from flying objects.

After Hurricane Alicia hit the coast of Texas, we lived for nine days without running water, electricity, and air conditioning in Houston's humidity and 105-degree heat, with two young children to care for. And then we watched as floodwaters came within six inches of our front door. Neighbors met in the middle of streets to navigate the floodwaters and look for victims to rescue.

When my husband was a reservist, we sat with others in his unit, glued to the TV, waiting for the activation call for Desert Storm and the cleanup detail after the bombing of the Federal Building in Oklahoma City.

Later we recalled these personal experiences as we watched the refugees of Kosovo flee their homeland to start new lives—without family members, without food, with only the clothes on their backs. The TV cameras recorded the images of strangers befriending those who were in greater need than they, becoming surrogate mothers, fathers, and friends to them.

Though the intensity of disasters and dangers may vary, the human spirit does not. From the inconvenient to the tragic, survivors' spirits reach out to others with concern and compassion that make difficult experiences bearable.

When others share our pain, our own load grows lighter.

Sometimes God's provision in time of trouble is our connection with one other person. Weak and discouraged, that person may disengage from the very source of help and hope. He or she may let go—of our hand, our help, our hope. Just as in times of physical disaster or injury, not everyone has the strength or the will to help themselves. At such times, another person's future may rest on our ability to hold on. Hold on, and then hold on longer.

■ ■ ■

This struggle of people against their conditions, this is where you find the meaning of life.

—ROSE CHERNIN

Life is not easy for any of us. But it is a continual challenge, and it is up to us to be cheerful and to be strong, so that those who depend on us may draw strength from our example.

—ROSE KENNEDY

Please Take Your Seats

There's nothing like 1,300 women trying to change seats "quickly and quietly" in a large auditorium to create a little disruption—and disgruntle more than a few. The occasion was a gathering of more than 18,000 women for a national women's conference in Sacramento. Just before the conference began on Friday evening, the director of the conference discovered, much to her dismay, that she had oversold 1,300 seats.

In a nutshell, that meant that when 2,600 women found their places in the large auditorium, fifty percent of them would be disappointed to find someone else seated there.

Of course, you must also consider that each displaced member of the audience had not come alone. That meant that those five or fifteen or fifty companions planning to be seated with her also faced a dilemma—should they grab any unoccupied adjoining seats or chance moving their whole group to a new location—and displace someone else, whose group would in turn be divided and disgruntled?

You get the picture. The hosts of the event trying to get everyone's attention to relay instructions about where to find open seating. Bodies, handbags, briefcases, and Bibles filling the aisles. Thirteen hundred women and their closest companions connected by their grumbling. Big delay in starting the program.

The grumbling continued through the welcome and opening announcements. Word came to the emcee already seated on the platform that she should say something in the way of an explanation or an apology. The purpose was to make things better, not worse. The emcee searched the tight schedule of speakers, trying to determine where an apology might be the least disruptive of the carefully planned transitions between topics and speakers.

Finally, she leaned over to the next speaker, Joni Eareckson Tada: "Joni, we've got a problem," she said and explained the cause of the 1,300 displaced and disgruntled women now roaming the aisles. "If you can think of something to say and it fits with what you'd planned to talk about, please mention the problem and offer an apology. If you can't think of how to work it in, then just don't worry about it. I'll figure out something sooner or later."

So Joni's turn to speak came, and she rolled her wheelchair up to the microphone. A quadriplegic since suffering a diving accident as a teenager, Joni offered this brief observation before launching into her prepared presentation. "I understand that there are some women here tonight who are not sitting in the seat they expected to be sitting in . . . So am I . . . And I know of thousands of people who would gladly trade seats with any one of you."

There's nothing like stark frankness to put things in perspective.

We should never measure our own misfortune by itself. If we do, it seems intolerable. But balanced against the suffering of the rest of humanity, ours most often is shown to be what it is: an inconvenience, not a catastrophe.

I'd received an e-mail from a lawyer friend earlier that morning, telling me about the behind-the-scenes scurrying to make things right at the conference. Knowing what these conference organizers were facing helped me put my latest quandary in perspective. I'd been worrying about how we would find the staff to cover all the training workshops we had scheduled over the next few months without two of our instructors. Reflecting on Joni's remark, I remembered past years during economic recessions when we had prayed for a predicament like the one we were now facing.

How easily we forget! Dissatisfaction, unchecked, is contagious. Like watered weeds, it grows until it overtakes a marriage, a workplace, or a mind. Perspective paves the way for prayers of gratitude rather than petition.

For I have learned to be content whatever the circumstances. I know what it is to be in need, and I know what it is to have plenty. I have learned the secret of being content in any and every situation, whether well fed or hungry, whether living in plenty or in want. I can do everything through him who gives me strength.

—PHILIPPIANS 4:11–13

Gratitude to God makes even a temporal blessing a taste of heaven.

—WILLIAM ROMAINE

He who forgets the language of gratitude can never be on speaking terms with happiness.

—C. NEIL STRAIT

Friends in Hard Places

I called my mother during a break in the trade show. "Do they have Daddy's test results yet?"

"Yes. They do. The doctor just left. He said there's a blockage in all four arteries—really in five places. He said most people have only four arteries to the heart, but some people have an abnormal, extra one. Like your dad. And that's the only one that's not blocked. He's got 98 percent blockage in all of the other four. The extra artery is the only one that's keeping him alive."

My heart was pounding so hard that I was afraid to take a breath. "So they're going ahead with surgery next week?"

"No. They're going to do it now. Today." Her voice was fearful, barely audible. "As soon as they can schedule an operating room. They take people in order of how critical their conditions are. The doctor just left to see if he can shuffle some patients around and get him into surgery immediately."

I hung up the phone and headed for the hospital. They did not get him into surgery until seven o'clock the next morning. By that time, the surgery waiting room was filled with more than thirty friends. Waiting. For whatever.

Several hours later, when the long surgery was done, the surgeon emerged to say that he thought my dad would be fine. The waiting room was still full.

But not for everyone. Other patients faced the same long surgery that day alone. My heart went out to them, knowing how much comfort my mom and we children had felt from having others there with us.

This is the thing: Pain can be halved when it is shared.

As Ralph Waldo Emerson observed, "The only way to have a friend is to be one." My parents have spent a lifetime depositing their concern in other people's lives, so when they needed to make a withdrawal, friends found them. There's nothing like a hospital stay to focus attention on the depth of relationships.

A friend of mine made the same observation about her own parents' circle of friends after they'd had a car accident. Before they were checked out and released from the emergency room, friends calling from all over the city jammed the hospital's switchboard for news of their condition.

Friends show up during the dark, difficult days.

A neighbor of mine learned this past spring not to make assumptions about the depth of relationships. For months, she'd been fighting a sinus infection and a lingering cough. She'd coughed, wheezed, sniffled, and sputtered for weeks. On April Fools' Day, she picked up her cell phone on a whim and dialed Bill, a man she'd been dating only two weeks. In a weak, whiny voice, she said, "I feel awful. I'm weak. I'm bleeding. I'm heading for the emergency room." She then paused, laughed, and added, "Just kidding. April fool. But checking into the hospital for a good *rest* does sound like an awfully good idea. See you this weekend."

Later that afternoon, she got a call from her mother, saying that Bill was trying to find her. Apparently he had not listened to the entire message; he'd hung up after the line about the emergency room and made a mad dash across the city to the hospital near her home. When he hadn't been able to find her at that hospital, he'd tried two other hospitals before calling her mother, who, of course, was in the dark about the whole incident.

When my neighbor called Bill at work to apologize and ask him to listen to the rest of her phone message, he told her he felt much like a parent who discovers his child has done something really dangerous and lived to tell about it. He vacillated between anger and relief.

But later, when telling me about the prank and her regret that she'd caused him so much trouble and worry, she reported one benefit: After his caring response, she did have a better indication of the depth of his interest in their relationship!

People's reactions to our difficulties paint pictures that stay with us.

In their eighties, my paternal grandparents could no longer take care of themselves at home. They decided to move into a nursing home because my grandmother, beginning to suffer from Alzheimer's disease, needed around-the-clock care. At first, my dad and mother encouraged them to consider a nursing home closer to the rest of the family so we all could visit more often and keep an eye on them. But my grandfather wouldn't hear of it. The friendships they had built throughout a lifetime meant too much to them. Their friends who were still able to walk or drive came to visit them every day at the nursing home for almost two years. Those priceless friendships kept them in that small town until their deaths.

In contrast, I attended a funeral of another relative some years ago. She and her husband, too, had lived in a small town for several years. Although they were both healthy and active, they did not make friends easily. They seemed self-sufficient. When the woman was suddenly overtaken by cancer, no one visited her, no one shared her burden, no one expressed concern. At her memorial service, there were ten people, including family members.

Such situations cause us to focus on the depth of our own relationships. The time for cultivating friendships is before you need them and before they need you.

Casual friends ask how you're feeling. Real friends can tell how you're feeling without asking.

Casual friends call you when they have time. Real friends call you even when they don't have time.

Casual friends talk to you about their problems. Real friends talk to you about your problems.

Casual friends send flowers to the hospital. Real friends bring you flowers—and work, books, letters, and anything else they can find to occupy your mind.

Casual friends ask what they can do for you. Real friends do things for you without asking.

Casual friends act like your guests. Real friends play host to everybody else.

Casual friends try to make you laugh. Real friends allow you to cry.

Casual friends say they'll pray for you. Real friends do.

Casual friends come and go. Real friends stay.

■ ■ ■

I have learned that to have a good friend is the greatest of God's gifts, for it is a love that has no exchange for payment.

—FANNIE FARMER

There is a friend who sticks closer than a brother.

—PROVERBS 18:24

If a man does not make new acquaintances as he advances through life, he will soon find himself alone. A man should keep his friendships in constant repair.

—SAMUEL JOHNSON

Be more prompt to go to a friend in adversity than in prosperity.

—CHILO

The friends who are the most stimulating to us are those who disagree with us. It is they whose ideas we should ponder.

—CORNELIA JAMES CANNON

Some Mother's Son

A young man of about twenty slipped into the back pew beside my husband and me one Sunday night during the worship service. During the greeting, I turned to shake his hand and introduce myself. In that brief exchange, I learned that he was originally from Louisiana and was now a recruit going through basic training at a nearby air base.

"Golly, I can't get over this," he said, glancing up at the ceiling and then side to side in the massive auditorium.

"What do you mean?" I asked.

"How big this place is. Far cry from the thirty or forty people we have in our church back home."

His Southern drawl was even thicker than mine, and his "gawl-leeee" sounded like Gomer Pyle.

"How do you ever get to know anybody around here?" he asked.

"You do. In small groups."

He nodded, and we rejoined the singing.

After the service, I turned to him and said, "I know you've probably got better things to do than hang around with a bunch of middle-aged married couples, but we're having a party at our house tonight. If you'd like to come . . ."

"You're inviting me without even knowing me?"

I smiled.

"Sure. How do I get there?" he said, all in one breath.

Once we arrived home with him safely in tow, we left him to mill among the other forty or so guests as we got snacks on the table. There was no one in the group under the age of thirty, but that didn't seem to bother this young man. He moved from cluster to cluster, introducing

"Well, my Billy's always been a hard worker. He's dependable. He's ambitious. You don't get a good job like that unless you've made a name for yourself."

"You got that right," her friend responded. "Well, you tell him that I'm mighty proud of him. That kind of good job doesn't come along every day."

"Yep," the mother agreed. "He's really done good for himself."

As a mother, I identified with the beam in her eye and the lilt in her voice. For parents, it comes with the territory.

Finally, parents share a common fear that children will be hurt. That's why moms and dads send valentines to every child in the class. That's why we choose the scrawny kid to light the candles on the birthday cake after we've noticed he was chosen last for sandlot baseball. That's why we forgive the sullen teenager next door for picking fights after we've learned that his dad just moved in with his mistress. That's why we take hand-me-downs to a friend's daughter who's just moved back to her parents' home with two school children and no means of support. We put judgments aside and act as any parent would to meet the emotional need.

Pride. Protection. Pain. Nothing reveals the nurturing nature of a mother more than the sight of her pride in the success of *someone else's* child, protecting *someone else's* child, or soothing the pain of *someone else's* child.

Motherhood connects us in our shared mission to change society one child at a time.

■ ■ ■

The soul is healed by being with children.

—FYODOR DOSTOEVSKY

What's done to children, they will do to society.

—KARL MENNINGER

Hours of Friendship

Jody and I knitted together a lifetime of friendship in a couple of days.

Her mother, Beadie, said casually one day to a small gathering of women at our church, "Our daughter's moving back home for a while and will be looking for a job here. If you hear of anything, please let us know." Between the lines, I read about a failed marriage and the loneliness of moving back to a small town to live with parents who had long enjoyed their empty nest after successfully launching two daughters into professional careers.

I could all too easily picture myself in the same situation. So I called Beadie, a replica of my own mother's petite size, godliness, and generous store of love. "I met Jody only briefly after the worship service Sunday, but I'm calling to see if she'd like to go shopping with me one day." Jody came on the line and accepted the invitation for herself.

We found ourselves sharing our lives over a four-hour lunch and a half-hour shopping spree. She told me her story briefly, not with self-pity but with a mixture of regret and resignation. She and her husband had been married only a few months when she discovered his self-loathing, his depression, and his violent temper. The day he tossed a cup of hot coffee in her face was the day she decided to exit the marriage.

Digging her way through mountains of guilt about divorce, she also wrestled with feeling that she'd disappointed her parents and dashed their hopes that she would have a happy marriage and children like her twin sister. As she told me her story, it seemed as if she were reading from my own diary. She shared my belief in the sacredness of marriage, my dreams of living happily ever after, and the financial burden of making a living. She, too, had supportive parents whom she felt she'd disappointed by choosing a mentally unstable husband. We finished our lunch that day as close as sisters.

On another day a few weeks later, we decided to have dinner and see a movie together. After we sat down to dinner and conversation, the movie plans never again entered our minds.

She soon found a nurse's job in a nearby city, and I started teaching school. Within a few months, we moved across the state from each other.

Three years later, my phone rang late in the afternoon. The voice seemed out of place but familiar. I racked my brain. Then I recognized the voice of Jody's father.

Thrilled to hear from him, I said, "James, I almost didn't recognize your voice. It must be all that peanut butter oatmeal you've been eating." That concoction had been a running joke since he and Beadie had become my friends during the many church youth camps we'd sponsored together.

"I'm calling with some bad news," he said. His tone was somber rather than teasing. "Jody was killed yesterday in a car accident on her way home." Then his voice broke, and my heart began to pound.

He continued through his tears, "She was doing so well, happy again, with her life back together."

"How? Something . . . A freak accident?" I knew I wasn't making sense, but he caught the drift.

"Drunk driver. He hit her head on. She died instantly." He lost control again; the pain was still too raw to allow him to talk further. He ended the brief phone call by saying, "I just wanted to let you know how much your friendship meant to her—your reaching out to her during the worst part of her life—when she was so lonely and her mother and I couldn't help her through it. Your friendship meant more to her than you'll know."

The truth was that we'd spent less than ten hours together. Had it seemed longer to her? I hoped so. It seemed like a lifetime to me.

When I hung up the phone, I felt like screaming, "No, no, you don't understand. She reached out to me." She let me share the nightmare I myself had been living through. My heart's connection with Jody for our brief ten hours of conversation provided the courage and strength to endure the next ten years. I had never told her of my gratitude, nor had she expressed the depth of her feeling for whatever comforting words I'd been able to share with her. We just knew. A connection like ours lasts a lifetime. And longer.

Friendship's true measure is not time but intensity—two souls joined in spirit, struggling for survival.

▪ ▪ ▪

Two persons love in one another the future good which they aid one another to unfold.

—MARGARET FULLER

It's entirely in your power to regulate the degree to which you peel back the layers of your personality when you disclose yourself to someone. You can keep that person on the surface, or you can allow her to penetrate, by degrees or directly, to that core.

—HARRIET BRAIKER

Oh the comfort, the inexpressible comfort of feeling safe with a person: having neither to weigh thoughts nor measure words, but to pour them out. Just as they are—chaff and grain together, knowing that a faithful hand will take and sift them, keep what is worth keeping, and then with the breath of kindness, blow the rest away.

—GEORGE ELIOT

A Tribute to the Talking Wounded

My friend Debi phoned me at the office late one afternoon. "You're not going to believe what just happened."

"What?" I asked.

"I just got fired."

"Why?"

"My supervisor said I just wasn't doing a good job—all this stuff about how I wasn't keeping everybody's schedule organized. That I had been off sick too much. That she had wanted to change things when she came in but that I wasn't cooperating—whatever that means. No good reason."

She burst into tears. "What am I going to do? How am I going to make it?"

"I'll be home in half an hour," I said. "Why don't you meet me there and we'll figure it all out."

Half an hour later, she rang my doorbell. Already her eyes were red and swollen, her blonde hair disheveled.

She came through the doorway talking and followed me into the kitchen, where most of our conversations usually take place. "How can she say I don't know how to do my job? I was doing a good job. I always got threes or above on my performance ratings with my other supervisor. Just call her—you can ask her. I always got threes.

"I don't know how I'm going to pay the bills. All I've got is *my* income. What are Bailey and I going to do?" She pointed to her twelve-year-old son, who'd come along with her. "I've got a $1,600 house payment. I've got a $548 car payment. We've got to eat. What am I going to do?

"My supervisor just didn't like me. But everybody else did. I have a great relationship with all the other people who work with me. They're always doing things for me. They love me. We have fun. I try to accommodate their schedules, and they do a good job helping me. We get along. Always threes.

"I don't get it—all of a sudden, after three years in the job—I've suddenly become incompetent?

"Nothing like kicking somebody when they're down, is there? She knew that I'm going through this divorce—that my husband left me for another woman. Doesn't she have any heart at all?

"What am I gonna do? How am I going to pay the bills? I'll never find another job. I don't have an education. I've never worked anywhere but at the nursery. I'm not too smart. You know me—I don't have good skills. I just can't learn things that fast. I haven't kept up with computers and all that. I can't spell all that well. What could I do? Who'd hire me?"

I continued to let her talk, responding only with nods and affirmations, hoping the ramble would help her work through the emotion of the moment.

"I guess I could apply out at Bell Helicopter. Someone mentioned a few weeks ago that they're hiring again. But I don't know what kind of chance I'd have. I guess you'd help me, wouldn't you? A reference or something?"

I nodded.

"And I could probably ask John. He works out there. He'd probably know somebody and could at least walk my application over to the right place and get it read. Wonder if they'd give me the same hours that I'm used to? I loved my hours at the nursery because I could get home before Bailey did." She again gestured toward her son who still stood by, listening to her monologue.

"I guess I could ask my mother to come live with me. Together we could make it. She needs me, too. For comfort. Bailey loves her."

Her son nodded in agreement.

"They have a great time together; they just *love* being together. I only hope mother will agree to it. She likes having her own place. But

I *need* her now. We all three would be a great help to each other. And she could help me pay for my house and sell hers. Do you think she'd do it?"

"I don't know. You'll just have to call and ask her," I said, trying to be helpful.

"Well, the first thing I thought when she called me into her office was, *Here we go—she's going to fire me.* And she did it! She said she was sorry to have to do it. I don't know, maybe she was. But she couldn't tell me *why.* I guess I have to give her the benefit of the doubt. Maybe her boss made her let me go. She really is a nice person.

"Whatever. I guess it's all immaterial now. I'm not even going to get to go back tomorrow. They had me clean out my desk before I left this afternoon. Can you believe that? That hurts. Makes me feel like I'm worthless, that they don't trust me anymore."

"That's pretty typical. Most companies do that with anybody they fire." Again, I tried to help her sort through the details.

"Maybe I could find a job as a dental hygienist. I used to do that. Long time ago. Before we were married. I guess I could start asking around."

She backed up against the kitchen cabinet and tossed the next comment heavenward. "Well, God, what are you going to do with me now? I just have to keep the faith that He has control of all this. That's what I always come back to. He knows that I've got to have a place to live and we've got to eat, right?

"And I've got to get over this croup I've had for the last four months. I just can't shake it. Cough, cough, cough. Hack, hack, hack. Fever every other day. I can't figure out what's going on with me. That probably has something to do with why I got fired. They're afraid I've got something contagious like tuberculosis. Who knows—maybe *that's* why she fired me. All threes and fours. Is she right? Did I just forget how to do my job suddenly when she became supervisor? Something's wrong with this picture."

I smiled my reassurance.

Her tears stopped. "Oh, well."

Then she took off in a different direction. "Poor Barb. She's in worse shape than I am. I've got to call her tonight and tell her what happened. She won't believe it either. Fired—can you believe that? Such a total shock. She walks in, she sits down, I'm fired . . . I need to go pick up flowers or some cookies to take to Barb. I think she's going to be looking for a new job, too."

She turned her face upward again. "Sometimes I just don't think I'll make it. But then I pray and read my Bible, and I know I'll make it somehow. We've just got to figure it out. I've got to take my time to think it all over and decide the best thing to do. God will get me through this—He always does. He has the answers; I just have to figure out how to understand them."

The intermittent tears stopped altogether. She thanked me for listening. I hugged her, and she and Bailey left.

As I watched her get back into her car, I considered what it is about her that makes me love and admire her. On the surface, we don't have much in common. She has a preteen; my children are grown. She has been a stay-at-home mom most of her adult life; I've worked outside the home most of mine. She prefers TV to books; I prefer books to TV. She plays tennis; I surf the Internet. I love to travel; she loves to stay home. She has very little interest in finance or business; I run my own company.

With all these differences, why am I drawn to her? She's unpretentious. She's candid. She's resourceful. She's unselfish. She's charitable. She's loyal. She has a positive attitude. She's appreciative. She trusts God's hand completely.

It suddenly struck me how useful to His kingdom God could make all of us, if we were all as transparent before Him about our weaknesses and dependency.

■ ■ ■

Humility is pride in God.

—Austin O'Malley

A man's pride brings him low, but a man of lowly spirit gains honor.

—Proverbs 29:23

If it's very painful for you to criticize your friends—you're safe in doing it. But if you take the slightest pleasure in it—that's the time to hold your tongue.

—Alice Miller

Planning and Presuming

Last summer, I received a note in the mail from an acquaintance I'd known briefly through our membership in the National Speakers Association. His hand-scribbled Post-it note was attached to an ad for one of my software packages that the producer had run in *USA Today*. The note said:

> Dear Dianna,
>
> This looks great—congratulations from an old friend! I have moved from Texas to Tennessee and now speak for one of my old clients on a full-time basis. It's fun and I love it . . . Hope we cross paths again along the way . . . God bless you!
>
> Dick Semaan

Attached to that note was a magazine article he'd written titled, "Bitter or Better: A Husband's Story about Breast Cancer." The article served to "catch me up" on his life since our paths had diverged ten years earlier in Houston. The article told of his surprise when he'd returned to his hotel room to see the blinking message light on his phone late one night. The message was from his wife, Sandra, telling him that she'd found a lump in her breast and that the doctor wanted her to come in for tests the following day. She had asked that he cut short his business trip and come home to be with her through the tests.

Tests confirmed that she had cancer. The article went on to describe their ordeal and how they had become stronger in the eight years since her first diagnosis. He had written the article in praise of his wife and her determination to become a better person in the midst of her struggle. The article included a photo of them arm in arm, looking forward to their future together. The article, I was sure, explained why

Dick had left his self-employed life, which entailed extensive travel, and had accepted the full-time job in Tennessee with a former client.

I immediately sent Dick a short note, thanking him for taking the time to write after so many years and wishing his wife continued good health.

About four weeks later, I received an e-mail from another colleague; it announced that Dick Semaan had just died from a massive heart attack. In the space of a month, I had connected with an old friend concerned about his wife's health, only to feel the shock of his sudden death.

Pulling Dick's earlier note from my file, I reread the article he'd penned. In it, he reaffirmed his wife's and his faith in God's plan for their lives. Gazing at the photo of the two of them, I recalled a conversation my husband and I'd had on a cruise to the Panama Canal the year before. On deck while waiting in a buffet line, we'd struck up a conversation with a spry older woman who seemed to be a veteran traveler.

"Yep, this is my twenty-seventh cruise," she beamed.

"No kidding—twenty-seven? Where have you been?" we asked. "Which cruise lines do you prefer?"

She proceeded to name her destinations and pass on her cruise-line ratings. "Want you to meet my friend Ellie," she gestured toward the woman in line behind her, and we shook hands. "I invited Ellie to come along and keep me company."

"Have you and Ellie made all twenty-seven cruises together?" we asked. Both women looked to be well into their eighties.

Ellie shook her head.

"No, this is the first time I've invited Ellie. I try to invite a different friend each year. Just makes me angry, though, every time I think about it."

"Angry?" we probed.

"Yeah. At my husband. We'd been saving all our life so that we could travel when he retired. Never could get him to take a vacation. He thought he couldn't leave his business. Then he finally retired when he was sixty-five. Made reservations for our first cruise. And if he didn't up and die on me four months later—before we ever went anywhere! So I just thought about it and decided I wasn't going to let that stop me. I've been inviting a different friend along every year since."

There's a fine, fuzzy line between planning and presuming. The Proverbs tell us that only the foolish give no thought to wise planning for the future. Yet the same Proverbs also warn us against presuming that God will grant us another day. The biblical injunction that tells us to "work because the night is coming" also embraces the concept of connection.

The bridge between the two habits, planning and presuming, lies in our attitude and activity during the wait. The wise don't wait until death stares them in the face to make the best decisions about living. Life is lived and relationships are shared somewhere between starting the plans and presuming the end.

■ ■ ■

Do not boast about tomorrow, for you do not know what a day may bring forth.

—PROVERBS 27:1

Commit to the LORD whatever you do, and your plans will succeed . . . In his heart a man plans his course, but the LORD determines his steps.

—PROVERBS 16:3, 9

Many are the plans in a man's heart, but it is the LORD'S purpose that prevails.

—PROVERBS 19:21

It's fantastic knowing you're going to die; it really makes having priorities and trying to follow them very real to you.

—SUSAN SONTAG

Death is simply a shedding of the physical body, like the butterfly coming out of a cocoon . . . It's like putting away your winter coat when spring comes.

—ELISABETH KUBLER-ROSS

Better Times

The eight-year-old admires his big brother as he speeds off in his Corvette to pick up a date. He can't wait until he has the freedom of a teenager—his own wheels, his own friends, and his own fun.

The teenager envies the college student, away from parents and home, who can call his own shots about curfews and career choices.

The college student bides his time in the classroom, eager to get into the "real world" of regular paychecks, respect, and corporate revolutions.

The thirty-something works to attain the security of an established career, complete with a new home, exotic vacations, and a savings account to cover the kids' college education.

The forty- to sixty-year-old worries about corporate downsizing, hoping to make it to that retirement cottage on the lake. She dreams of time for hobbies and freedom from the day-to-day stresses of aging parents and still-dependent children.

The senior, fearing that he has nothing meaningful to contribute and shackled by a tired body, longs once again to have the energy and opportunities of an eight-year-old.

Each decade looks different on the front end. So we label the upcoming one "better"—until we get there.

That same thinking prevails on the job. The warehouse clerk wants to be in management, where the big perks and power rest. But the manager drags herself home at night with a briefcase full of paperwork, toying with the idea of going back to a "simpler" job that would allow more time off with the kids.

We think similar thoughts about relationships. When we're feeling lonely, we long for intimate friendships; when we're feeling put upon by a friend's demands, we wish the relationship were less intense. Married couples sometimes want the freedom and choices that come with being single; singles often want the security and companionship of a marriage partner.

Citizens go through the same gyrations with their government. They long for the good old days of low unemployment and lower taxes, but they want the services provided by the latest tax levied on the neighbor's business. The only thing that changes when politicians run for office is the era that is labeled "the good old days."

"Better times" has become synonymous with "other times."

Maybe the restlessness that colors the current age, job, relationship, or era stems from ingratitude. Our egos say we deserve more or better than we're currently enjoying. Every reward that comes our way counts only as a teaser for what we "should" earn further down the line.

Or maybe we have unrealistic expectations of the future. We assume that the future implies advancement or improvement. Not necessarily so. Only a few years ago, corporations came to grips with the fact that an engineer's reward for excellent performance is not necessarily a promotion to manager. It may simply mean more years as an engineer. For the first time in history, we're raising a generation of people who may have less than their parents did.

Some people define "better" as having what the neighbors have. And they've seen so many Hollywood movies that they assume the rags-to-riches story should be lived by everyone. But that logic is based on the notion that those who *have* more *feel* happier. These people live their lives thinking, "I'll be happy when . . ."

Whether tomorrow is uphill, downhill, or straight ahead, life happens while we're on the way to the end. Life is a direction and a duration, not a destination.

Maybe all we need to do to live in better times is to change our outlook on the present. Every now and again, life backs up on us, and everything looks snarled through the windshield. Gratitude to God and connection to others eliminates the road noise, cuts through the congestion, and gives us perspective. You can't be content without connecting.

■ ■ ■

For I have learned to be content whatever the circumstances.

—PHILIPPIANS 4:11

If you can't be content with what you have received, be thankful for what you have escaped.

—UNKNOWN

It is not how much we have, but how much we enjoy, that makes happiness.

—CHARLES SPURGEON

By the time a man finds greener pastures, he's too old to climb the fence.

—UNKNOWN

Do not anxiously hope for what is not yet come; do not vainly regret what is already past.

—CHINESE PROVERB

Everything happens to everybody sooner or later if there is time enough.

—GEORGE BERNARD SHAW

Most people think they would rather be miserably rich than happily poor.

—UNKNOWN

As Any Mother Knows

As luck would have it, Vicky had been booked to shoot her latest talk show during the one week of the entire semester—spring break—in which she couldn't arrange a sitter. Well, bored or not, her son Timmy would have to tag along. But reminding herself how lucky she was that her boss never complained when one of her boys accompanied her to the studio during a minor emergency, she rushed Timmy through breakfast and headed off to work.

Even though she wasn't a full-time employee, Vicky suspected that her colleagues would plan a typical birthday "surprise" gathering for her about midafternoon. Balloons tied to her dressing room door. A cake sporting some cliché about being over the hill. A card signed with the wittiest remark each coworker could come up with on twenty seconds' notice.

When she arrived on the set, her coworkers feigned a cool indifference—the typical birthday ploy. She shuffled Timmy into a corner of the makeup studio so he could play with the puzzle he'd brought along while the stylist did her makeup and hair. Then into the studio they traipsed, where she took her place on the set as co-host of the talk show. Timmy settled into the shadows to watch. Even though he'd been on the set several times in his young life, the crew—with their cameras, special lighting effects, moving cranes, and funny lingo—captured his attention.

They finished by midafternoon. So far, so good with Timmy in tow. It had been easier to keep him entertained than she had thought it would be.

As soon as Timmy heard, "It's a wrap," he darted from his perch in the shadows. "Hey, Mom, what happened? You had to do five takes about the motorcycles! What happened to you, huh?"

Vicky swatted at his denim bottom. "You made me nervous, that's what."

"Your tongue got tangled?"

"Yep," she played along. "It was that peanut butter I ate last night."

"I knew all about that motorcycle story, Mom. Could I go next time you shoot a story on cycles?"

"That's not my deal," she brushed his exuberance aside. "Ready to go home?"

"Wait, wait," the floor director called to her, pointing to his headset. "They've changed their minds in the control room. It's not a wrap yet. Just hang around here a minute and see what we've got to redo."

Within seconds, several coworkers appeared in the studio wings, and she got the drift. Then in walked the bearer of the cake to confirm it. Timmy looked delighted to be part of the action. She took his hand and introduced him to several of her coworkers while they decided who was going to cut the cake and if "everyone" was present yet. Her male co-host obviously had been aware of the appointed time and stood by, sporting a sheepish grin. He introduced his wife, Elizabeth, who also happened to be on the set for the taping.

The crowd began a slightly off-key round of "Happy Birthday." Just as they finished, Vicky's boss stepped to the center of the hoopla and said, "Vicky, since this is a special birthday year and since you're still single and searching for the perfect man . . ." he paused, as if for a drumroll.

Vicky could feel herself redden. She and her boss enjoyed a good working relationship, but he seemed to catch her off guard quite often with his dry wit and practical jokes. She never quite knew what he might come out with. Although he knew she was a Christian, he rarely let her idea of right and wrong inhibit his own life style.

To the crowd gathered around her and Timmy, the boss continued in his emcee voice, "So since Vicky is definitely getting up in years and still hasn't found the man of her dreams, we've decided to help her along."

Suddenly the PA system began to blare "The Stripper." Then the studio door opened, and in bolted a male stripper.

Vicky turned beet red. Timmy's eyes grew wide as he stared first at her and then the doorway. She squeezed Timmy's hand and glanced toward the exit doors. What to do? They were surrounded by laughter and squeals. How could she protect him from this scene?

As if reading her mind, her newfound acquaintance, Elizabeth, stepped out of the crowd. "Why don't you come with me, Timmy? This party's going to get awfully boring. How about some ice cream?"

"Can I, Mom?" he yelled over the music, oblivious to what was about to transpire onstage.

With eyes gratefully locked on Elizabeth's, Vicky quickly nodded her permission, and they were gone.

Sooner or later, all parents feel a touch of sadness when they must tell or confirm to their children the news that there is no Easter bunny, Santa Claus, or tooth fairy. But parents have learned to dilute their children's disappointment with the assurance that the love that spawned these myths is real.

The tougher assignment is to explain to children the *depraved* nature of humanity. Yet that discussion may stay with a child much longer than the truth about the tooth fairy.

In a split second, Elizabeth and Vicky connected through their common bond of motherhood, the instinct to shield an innocent child from the world, if only for a few seconds.

■ ■ ■

The more things a man is ashamed of, the more respectable he is.
—GEORGE BERNARD SHAW

The age of discretion is when you make a fool of yourself in a more dignified way.

—UNKNOWN

Nothing worries a parent more than the uneasy feeling that his children are relying more on his example than his advice.

—UNKNOWN

A hurtful act is the transference to others of the degradation which we bear in ourselves.

—SIMONE WEIL

Train a child in the way he should go, and when he is old he will not turn from it.

—PROVERBS 22:6

Things Look the Same
in the Emergency Room

The admission window and nurse. Scrubbed, shiny floors. The smell of alcohol. The chill of refrigerated air. The sterile gleam of silver instruments. Hours of tedium in the waiting room. In addition to facing fear, pain, and possibly death, a patient in an emergency room also has to deal with the irritating reality of long lines.

My daughter had called our office en route to the hospital with my two-year-old grandson, who was having difficulty breathing. My son-in-law was out of town; I was out of town; and Vernon, her stepdad, was next in line. Although it was not their first trip to the hospital at high speed, a new asthma attack still stirred panic. Vernon met them at the emergency room a half-hour later.

The nurses rushed Mason into an examining room and began a breathing treatment shortly after the doctor on call had seen him. After his ordeal under the mask, Mason was taken back to the lobby for a few hours of waiting to see if the treatment was sufficient or if he would have to be admitted to the hospital.

As Lisa, Mason, and my husband returned to the waiting room, they noticed that a Hispanic woman who had been sitting there with her baby when they'd first arrived was still waiting. They spoke to her briefly and took a seat in the corner, away from the hubbub of others coming and going.

As the afternoon wore on, Mason grew more restless and whiny. An hour passed. Vernon went to the cafeteria to grab a hamburger because he'd missed his lunch. When he returned, he tried to entertain Mason while Lisa took her turn in the cafeteria. She returned with Jell-O and milk but could not interest Mason in either.

Two more hours passed. Patients came and went.

The Hispanic woman still sat across the room, with her tiny baby cradled in her arms. The baby cried and slept intermittently. The woman looked weary, sad, alone. Vernon walked over to her and said, "Ma'am, how long have you been waiting?"

"Since early this morning," she said in broken English.

"Have you seen a doctor yet?"

"No. Nurse says she's taking more serious cases first."

"But it's five o'clock—have you eaten anything today?"

She shook her head.

"Are you expecting anybody to come—to help you with the baby?"

Once again, she shook her head.

"Would you like me to get you something to eat and bring it back here?"

She nodded, and her eyes filled with tears. Vernon left and returned with a dinner tray for her. Then he asked the admitting nurse why the baby hadn't been seen yet by a doctor. Within minutes, the nurse called the Hispanic woman and baby into an examining room.

When Vernon called my hotel room later in the evening to tell me about the day, he mentioned the woman and her baby. I could easily imagine the scene from a mother's perspective. The fear of not knowing how sick the tiny baby was. The fatigue from hours of soothing a crying baby. The loneliness of not fully understanding the language. The anxiety of endless waiting. My husband must have seemed like an angel of mercy to her.

In times of sickness and death, differences that sometimes divide disappear. When my family and that of the Hispanic woman left the hospital hours later, they were no longer strangers; they had connected through their love for a sick child, the need for solace, and the resources of a Savior.

Kind words can be short and easy to speak, but their echoes are truly endless.

—MOTHER TERESA

You cannot do a kindness too soon, because you never know how soon it will be too late.

—UNKNOWN

Whatever you did for one of the least of these brothers of mine, you did for me.

—MATTHEW 25:40

Why Do Things Always
Look Better in the Morning?

I've gone to bed angry enough to move out of the school district and awakened with plans to add another room to the house. I've gone to bed pouting about something my husband has done and awakened planning a surprise birthday party for him. I've been sick enough at midnight to call an ambulance and awakened feeling fit and ready to go to work. In the wee hours, I've made a firm decision to investigate bankruptcy proceedings and awakened ready to shop for a new pair of shoes.

What is it about the morning that gives the discouraged new hope, the weak more strength, the defeated new inspiration?

For one thing, life's rituals train us to wake up to action in the morning. As babies, our parents lift us out of the crib for food and play. As children, we get up and dress to go to school. As adults, we get up and dress to go to work. We are trained to know that action follows the night's inertia. We connect with others who have plans and purpose for the day.

For another thing, we are tempted by the atmosphere around us. As the rest of the world wakes up, sounds increase as others hustle and bustle about their business. We realize they have people to see, places to go, business to do.

For another thing, the morning sunlight serves as an analogy for new beginnings. Whatever happened yesterday is gone; the mistakes are behind us. The sunlight spells a new day for new connections, new undertakings, new insights, new resolutions, new hope.

Finally, we're rested. Much like a car that spits and sputters on a cold morning, when we shake off our physical sluggishness, our mental motors start to purr.

It's morning. God is on his throne. There's sunlight. There's movement. There's time.

■ ■ ■

Evening, morning and noon I cry out in distress, and he hears my voice.

—Psalm 55:17

I find the great thing in this world is, not where we stand, but in what direction we are moving.

—Oliver Wendell Holmes

Reunions

Last year seemed to be our year for reunions. I was invited to both a high school reunion and a college reunion. My husband was invited to his high school, college, and fraternity reunions. I went to a family reunion of the great-aunts and great-uncles. He went to a family reunion of first cousins. We even had a reunion of former members of our home church. So during the year of reconnecting with friends and family members, I began to consider how reunions here on earth are much like I expect they'll be in heaven.

You go to the mailbox and say, "Hey, look at this—an invitation to our class reunion! Oh, but it's not until August. Gee, I wish it were this next weekend. After all these years, I hate to have to wait until August to see everybody. I'm ready to see them *now*."

Sounds unlikely, doesn't it? The more typical reaction, after realizing that ten or twenty years have gone by so quickly, is to grab the calendar and start counting the weeks. "If I start a diet tomorrow, I could possibly lose twenty pounds by then." Or "I've been meaning to change jobs for the last couple of years—do you think I could find something more glamorous in the next few weeks?"

No matter when the invitation arrives in the mail and no matter in whose mailbox it lands, I have a hunch that nearly everyone wants to be better prepared to see former classmates and old friends.

I'm inclined to think that's how it's going to be when we all get to heaven. "You know, there were just a few more things I intended to do before I arrived at these pearly gates. I was going to try to get things patched up with Katherine. She hurt my feelings back in 1998—a little thing that really didn't amount to much. I was planning to call her someday and suggest lunch so we could put it all behind us. And that senior citizen program on Sunday afternoons—I was going to practice the piano a little more and then volunteer to play for the seniors when I learned a few more hymns. And my prayer time— at the beginning of the new year, I was planning to stretch that to fifteen minutes a day. That reminds me about my grandson—I intended to spend a little more time with him. And my coworker Michelle—I had planned to sit down with her and talk about my faith sometime soon."

I can imagine that a great many people arriving at that heavenly reunion will wish they'd been better prepared. I can almost hear it now: "Lord, I intended to forgive more people and give more money to the ministry and tell a few friends how they could trust in You and . . ."

Here's a second similarity between earthly and heavenly reunions: Everyone won't be there. At my high school reunion, someone posted a list of the names of classmates who'd died in the intervening years, several in the Vietnam War, others in car accidents, a few from illness. I remember staring at the list and seeing the name Jennifer Newbern there, along with the date of her death, only two or three years after graduation. Someone said she'd been killed in a car accident. I could still visualize her seated beside me in speech class. Long, silky, red hair parted down the middle and hanging almost to her waist. Fair complexion. Big blue eyes. She had been rich—the rest of us referred to her house as the castle on Fielder Road. Dead. We never expected it.

And then there were those who simply chose not to attend for a variety of reasons or for no reason at all. I had hoped to see Sandra, a close friend when we were high school seniors. We'd drifted apart in college. Somebody told me she'd said that she "didn't have any reason" to attend the reunion. I was disappointed.

The same is true of our heavenly reunion: Everyone won't be there. Some won't be there by choice. Some will have had good intentions but delayed until it was too late. Some will find they'd been deceived by listening to people who gave them the wrong directions. Others will have understood the way without seeing a need or urgency to prepare.

The element of surprise is a third factor present at most reunions.

At my high school reunion, I discovered that shy Marcia had become an assertive corporate lawyer. David, formerly an overweight geek, was now a CEO of a large biotech conglomerate. Baton-twirling JoBeth had become a movie actress. The handsome and fit quarterback had turned into a plumber with a paunch.

Our heavenly reunion may be filled with similar surprises. The superstar evangelist may have gotten his rewards here on earth, while the unknown pastor in the trenches may be wearing the garlands in heaven. The elderly neighbor who always took time to listen to troubled teens after school may be hearing, "Well done, good and faithful servant," while the soloist with five best-selling albums may be hardly recognizable to the crowds at heaven's gate.

Lack of preparation. Absences. Surprises. Reunions can connect us—and they can separate us. If we learn from the earthly reunions, maybe we'll be better prepared for the heavenly ones in the hereafter.

■ ■ ■

There is a way that seems right to a man, but in the end it leads to death.

—Proverbs 14:12

In my Father's house are many rooms; if it were not so, I would have told you. I am going there to prepare a place for you. And if I go and prepare a place for you, I will come back and take you to be with me that you also may be where I am.

—John 14:2–3

We who are still alive and are left will be caught up together with them in the clouds to meet the Lord in the air. And so we will be with the Lord forever.

—1 Thessalonians 4:17

Life Is Uncertain; Get to the Main Performance Early

They call them warmup bands, those lesser-known groups that take the stage to warm up the crowd for the star, who will perform later. I guess the assumption is that the longer you wait for the real attraction, the greater your anticipation and enjoyment will be. But what happens if you have to go to the bathroom just about the time the real star comes on? By the time you make your exit and stand in line for a stall, you will have missed most of the show.

It's the same with books and movies. You invest hours reading those long passages about the leaves falling across the lawn in the twilight, reading toward a purpose or conclusion. Ten o'clock. Eleven o'clock. Midnight. You push on, turning page after page to discover who done it. Then your spouse walks in and asks, "Did you get to the part where Margo has a heart attack after she shoots John?" So much for suspense.

The same thing happens with cooking and company. My daughter phoned to ask if she could bring friends home with her from college to spend the weekend, arriving in time for Friday night dinner.

"Sure," I said. "Who's coming? How many?"

"About twelve. Or maybe twenty. I don't know exactly. I think maybe ten couples. Or could be only six couples. They haven't all told me for sure."

I swallowed. OK, twenty nineteen-year-olds for the weekend. My first thought? Food.

"Mickey may or may not bring a date," she rambled on. "And I don't know for sure about Angel and her boyfriend. I figure the guys can sleep downstairs in the game room and we girls will take the upstairs. See, we've got this fraternity deal in Dallas on Saturday, and so . . ."

As I listened to her ramble on about their weekend plans, my mind raced toward my to-do list. I'd be flying in late Thursday night. That meant that on Friday, I'd finish the vacuuming. Check clean sheets for the extra beds. Do our laundry early in order to turn the washing machine over to our visitors for their nonstop use. Get plenty of snacks for midnight.

I spent two days marinating the beef and preparing the raspberry cream-cheese salad, the squash casserole, and the yeast rolls. For dessert: chocolate crepes topped with cream, pecans, and cherries.

By the time I served these dishes, I was too tired to swallow. My daughter and her friends laughed and played while I sat limply, looking on from the sidelines. Had I ordered out for pizza, they'd have been just as happy to be together under the same roof, and I'd have enjoyed the fun as a participant rather than an exhausted observer.

I never connected; I only watched.

Life's like that. You put in twenty years in the hope of taking over the division, and then, once you're named director, you hear that the division is being restructured and your title no longer carries clout. You spend four years earning an undergraduate degree and six more years earning advanced degrees only to move into the business world and discover there's a glut of similar specialists, all vying for a shrinking number of jobs. You spend months or years decorating your dream house, and then you or your spouse is transferred across the country to another job.

People go away. Jobs disappoint. Money disappears. Do you ever have the feeling that you'll never make it to the best part of life? That you'll never find the job that will really fulfill you? That you'll never quiet the turmoil deep inside until you write that poem or that play? That you'll never have peace until you talk to that friend about your faith?

I figure you should do whatever you want to do—the most meaningful thing—each morning when you wake up. And then work backward throughout the day. God calls that purpose.

■ ■ ■

Some things are very important, and some are very unimportant. To know the difference is what we are given life to find out.
—ANNA F. TREVISAN

I don't want to be a passenger in my own life.
—DIANE ACKERMAN

Investment Strategies for Life

Several years ago I was leading a series of seminars at a management-consulting firm. During the planning meeting with a group of six regional managers, someone suggested a networking event the evening before the daylong seminar. They asked me to deliver an after-dinner speech as part of that networking event.

I agreed, asking which of my speech topics they'd prefer. "Since you're going to be talking heavy business stuff—the gender-communication and management issues—the next day, why don't you do something light for the after-dinner speech?"

"OK. How about something on keeping personal balance in your life?"

"That sounds fine," they agreed, almost absent-mindedly. "We need that for sure—everybody needs more balance. Work is killing us." And they rushed on to discuss other decisions and plans.

So I showed up at the networking dinner and gave the talk, using humorous anecdotes to illustrate each point. But the laughter was subdued. In fact, the further I got into the talk, the quieter the audience grew. As I plodded on, the audience grew even more pensive. In fact, expressions seemed pained, even hostile, by the time I finished. It was the longest forty-five-minute speech I've ever delivered.

After I took my seat at my table of ten, one of the women leaned over to me and said, "That was a nice job. But kind of ironic that they'd have you speak on that topic."

"Ironic?" I probed. I was glad to hear any explanation she offered.

"Yeah. If you work for our company, you don't have a personal life, period. They don't allow it. Most of us work eighty or ninety hours a week. Balance—why would they pick a topic like that?"

The others at the table chimed in, confirming her comments about the organization's culture. Then they began to trade stories of heroic feats and long hours that required all their emotional strength and physical stamina just to keep their heads above water.

Later in the evening, as I was leaving the meeting room, another woman stopped me. "You made some really valid points, but I guess you could tell that most of us here couldn't even identify with the stories you were telling. Did you know that out of this group of more than one hundred women, only four are married? And they don't have kids. Our life is work. Period. There's just no time for other relationships. Your talk made me kind of sad about what I'm missing in life."

Then as someone else approached us, her expression changed and her tone artificially brightened. She continued, "But it's an investment. The money's good. The first few years here are strictly an investment in your career."

As I flew home the following day, I turned her words over in my mind. She'd called her life style an investment. How and when did she measure the return?

When you buy stocks, you expect to see a return on your money within a reasonable period. Whether you check the earnings once a week or once a year, you want to see that return inching upward.

When you land a new job and work hard at it, you want to be rewarded. You want to be given more, or at least more challenging, responsibilities. You expect a merit raise.

When you spend money and time on a direct-mail blitz for a fund-raising campaign, you want to see those donations pour in within days.

But, unlike expectations in these other areas of life, investing in kids does not always result in immediate returns. Unlike the stock market, character doesn't go up or down overnight. As a parent, you'll put in about 3,285 hours reading bedtime stories, 72 hours walking through museums, 240 hours attending Little League games, 180 hours making medical visits, 36 hours applauding at school plays, 936 hours attending church or synagogue, 10,226 hours answering questions, 68 hours doling out and enforcing discipline, and 3,024 hours on family outings . . . before you'll see much of a trend at all.

In fact, you may not read your success as a parent until you see the lives your kids lead as adults.

Talking is not necessarily connecting. Far too many parents talk *at* their kids rather than *with* them. They tell them what time to be home, where they can or can't go, how much money they can or cannot spend. But beyond those minimal exchanges, they have no real connection. They merely exist under the same roof.

What does real connection cost?

Several years ago Don, a father of two teenage boys, made a strong impression on me after a discussion in which he told me he had planned a business trip for the following Monday morning. He told me he would be in Atlanta attending meetings all week and would see us the following weekend. But to my surprise, I bumped into him at a Little League game on Thursday evening.

"You must have made a strong presentation this week," I said to him at the concession stand.

"What do you mean?"

"Home a day early from Atlanta—you must have gotten them to sign on the dotted line sooner than you had expected."

"Oh, that," he shrugged. "No, I've gotta fly back early in the morning to finish up."

"So why did you come home in the middle of the week? Is something wrong?"

"No. Rich is pitching," he said as if that explained everything.

Connecting with your kids takes commitment. From birth. It's no wonder that Don's boys grew up to be strong men of faith and family. The best thing that parents can spend on their children is time—not money.

If your financial investment strategy is to buy blue-chip stocks and hold them forever, you'll probably feel comfortable investing time in your kids. Otherwise, you might consider selling them before they get out of diapers.

Love the LORD your God with all your heart and with all your soul and with all your strength. These commandments that I give you today are to be upon your hearts. Impress them on your children. Talk about them when you sit at home and when you walk along the road, when you lie down and when you get up.

— DEUTERONOMY 6:5–7

The trouble with being a parent is that by the time you're experienced, you're usually unemployed.

— UNKNOWN

What's in a Name?

I see they finally gave you an office at Chevron," an engineering friend said to me years ago after I'd started my consulting business in Houston.

"Not unless they forgot to tell me about it!" I responded.

"Then did you know you have a twin? I was walking down the hall out there last week and saw your name on a door. I actually almost burst in to say hello before I discovered it wasn't you. I figured you were working there on a consulting project."

I shrugged it off, but the fact that there are two people—even in a city the size of Houston—with the name Dianna Booher surprised me. After all, the name is not as common as Mary Smith, Cathy Jones, or Tom Williams.

Then I was reminded of an embarrassing moment that had occurred about ten years earlier in college. The English Comp 101 teaching assistant had been stumbling through the roster on the first day of class, then looked up and said, "Dianna Booher? Didn't you take this class last semester?"

"No, I didn't." Mortified that my classmates would think I'd failed the class the first time around, I slid down in my seat.

"Are you sure?" the TA persisted. "I'm sure I remember having a Dianna Booher on the roll last fall."

"Well, it wasn't me," I said again, more firmly.

A couple of years passed. One Saturday afternoon I received a strange but welcome call. "Is this Dianna Booher?" the caller asked frantically.

"Yes, it is."

"Thank goodness." The voice seemed to relax. "This is Rachel

Ginsburg. I've been trying to reach you all morning to give you the last-minute details of your itinerary on Monday."

I breathed a sigh of relief. I was to begin an author tour and didn't yet have all the details about an early-morning TV show scheduled for Monday. "I'm sorry you had trouble reaching me, but I've been home all morning."

"No, it's not your fault. It's just that I didn't have your home phone number with me and couldn't get back to my office to get it." She explained that a severe snowstorm in New York City had caused the publisher to close the offices early on Friday and send everyone home in a hurry. She'd been hoping to get my number by calling directory assistance, but eight Boohers were listed, and the operator would give her only three numbers at a time.

On the second group of three, Rachel had thought she was in luck. When she called the number and asked if she had the correct number for *Dianna* Booher, the woman who answered verified that, yes, she was indeed *Dianna* Booher. It took only a couple of minutes, however, to discover that this was not the *correct* Dianna Booher.

Needless to say, Rachel was relieved when she finally reached me. The other Dianna Booher had been kind enough to pull out the Houston phone directory and give Rachel the numbers of the remaining Boohers in the book.

Rachel and I had a good laugh over the coincidence. Before she hung up, she gave me the phone number of the other woman, suggesting that we trade key information in case we got each other's calls or correspondence again.

I gave the other woman a call. She laughed when I stated my name and described the earlier confusion. We decided to find out what else we might have in common.

We discovered that we had both married men with the same first name. We both had a brother by the same name. We both had extended family in Oklahoma. That, she said, explained why she had received a letter the previous year inviting her to a family reunion in Oklahoma—from someone whose name she didn't recognize, talking about relatives she didn't know! We traded phone numbers and addresses and never heard from each other again. Until . . .

My company was hosting a business-writing workshop in our own training facility fifteen years later. An attendee stepped into my office during a coffee break. He introduced himself. "Although we've never met," he said, "I'll be attending your daughter's wedding. We know the groom. My wife and I are friends of the family."

I smiled and nodded but certainly didn't expect his next revelation.

"By the way, we had a little confusion when we called Foley's department store to order china or crystal or whatever it is that my wife bought them for a wedding present."

"Really? What confusion?"

"Did you know that there's another Lisa Booher in the area? Marrying a guy with the same first name, Kevin? And both couples are getting married on August 7?"

"Too weird," was all I could muster. "That's just too weird." I went on to explain the earlier connections. Could this same person have moved along with me to Dallas? What were the odds?

Since the time of that discovery, I bought furniture at a store in Dallas. The clerk keyed my name into the computer to bring up my account number. "OK, I've got it," the sales associate said. "Dianna Booher. Let me just verify the address for delivery. You're on Elmhurst?"

"No."

"Change of address?" she asked.

"No. Same address. Different Dianna Booher." I gave her my address, and she located my account.

Six months later, I switched a prescription to a new pharmacy.

"OK, let me verify your address for insurance records. Still on Elmhurst?"

"No."

"Change of address?"

"No. Same address. Different Dianna Booher."

"Your name's not all that common," the pharmacist said. "That's a coincidence, isn't it, that you're having a prescription filled at the same pharmacy?"

I smiled and started to tell him the rest but then decided he wouldn't believe it.

Since the last two revelations, I've been thinking about my ongoing connection with this woman, whom I've never met in person. When I was a teenager still living with my parents, I recall hearing my dad take a few calls from people demanding payment on a big debt. The other guy by the same name was an auto mechanic who evidently owed a lot of money to a lot of people. The calls were not pleasant.

These incidents caused me to think about name-doubles in our technologically wired world. Consider the business we transact each year by phone, fax, and the Internet—all without ever meeting the people with whom we're doing business.

What if you were connected to another person by a shared name? What if you had the name of Bill Gates? Hillary Clinton? Michael Jordan? How many doors would open for you if you phoned someone to ask for a favor? On the other hand, what if you shared the same name as unabomber Theodore Kaczynski, Yugoslav leader Slobodan Milosevic, or former White House intern Monica Lewinsky? How many people would be put off, distrustful, fearful, or even contemptuous?

Bearing the same name, we could certainly create a lot of trouble or embarrassment for each other, should one of us turn out to be an unsavory character. Defunct companies. Calls from masquerading relatives about altered wills and loans. Bad publicity. Damaged credit ratings. Legal difficulties and even mistaken arrest records. Ruined reputations. What a nightmare that connection could be!

A lot of people have created similar confusion about the label Christian. They wear the name but practice a different life style. Cassie Bernall lost her life in the Columbine school shooting in Littleton, Colorado, because she said "yes" to the killer's question about whether she believed in God. A note was left near the cross commemorating her life and commitment. It said, "It's nice to finally see a Christian who lived up to the name."

If someone else bore your name and decided to impersonate you, would your name open or close doors? Wearing the name Christian, do you clarify for or confuse others about the Christ, the cause, and the commitment?

■ ■ ■

Authentic Christianity never destroys what is good. It makes it grow, transfigures it, and enriches itself from it.

—CLAIRE HUCHET BISHOP

There are always two choices. Two paths to take. One is easy, and its only reward is that it's easy.

—ANONYMOUS

Mail in My Box

You've probably seen some of those signs that hang in novelty shops:

"You don't have to be crazy to work here—but it helps!"

"Customer service rules: Rule #1: The customer is always right. Rule #2: When the customer is wrong, see Rule #1."

"As soon as I find time, I'm going to have a nervous breakdown."

"Is this a major crisis, or do I have time to get a cup of coffee?"

We chuckle at these signs because they so adequately describe the frantic pace most of us keep every day. That explains why we often fail to take the time to connect with our customers and clients on a personal level. It *explains* that failure—but it doesn't *excuse* it.

Fortunately, many people do wake up each morning anticipating that they'll meet people during the day who need their cheer and assistance.

Belinda, one of our consultants, flew to Denver to conduct a customer service communication class for IBM systems-support people. For some logistical reason that I've long since forgotten, she was staying at a small hotel, the Gun Barrel Inn, on the outskirts of the city. When she emerged from the hotel at about six o'clock the first morning of class, she discovered that she'd locked her keys inside the rental car. Although she had planned to arrive at least an hour before the class was scheduled to begin, this development could cause her to be late for the class itself. She rushed back inside to the phone near the small registration counter. She phoned the rental-car company only to be told that no one would be available to help her for at least a couple of hours. Panic rising, she grabbed the yellow pages in search of a locksmith.

"Excuse me," the hotel manager called to her from the registration counter. "I couldn't help but overhear your conversation with the rental-car company. I have an idea: Would you like to take my car for the day? I just came to work, and I won't be needing it today."

Belinda's jaw dropped. "But . . . you don't know me."

"But I understand the predicament." The manager pulled her purse out of the drawer underneath the counter and held out her car keys.

"But I may not be back until after six o'clock tonight—will you still be here?"

"I'll still be here. I'm not planning to go anywhere all day."

Gratefully, Belinda took the manager's car. The story became her opening illustration of excellent customer service in the workshop. Guess where all our instructors always stay when they go to Denver? Guess how many people around the country have heard the story about that excellent hotel?

Unfortunately, all hotel managers don't have that way of connecting with their customers. Only a few months ago, I finished a meeting in Portland early in the morning and returned to my hotel for a couple of hours before my flight was to leave. The person at the front desk explained that the hotel's shuttle would be leaving every half-hour and that the driver would come into the lobby to announce his departure. I relaxed a moment with a cup of hot tea and watched people come and go. After a few minutes, a nice-looking couple in their midthirties dressed in resort wear breezed in, waved to the people behind the front desk, took a couple of rolls and coffee from the breakfast buffet, and yelled to one of the bellmen, "Let's go."

I continued to wait as other guests checked out at the front desk and headed for their rental cars or climbed into the cars of colleagues.

My flight time was getting closer. I asked again when the shuttle would leave for the airport. The desk clerk checked his watch. "There won't be another shuttle for a half-hour."

"What happened to the one at ten o'clock? When I asked earlier, you said there would be a shuttle every half-hour and that the driver would come in to announce when he was leaving."

"Well, the shuttle just left," the clerk said. "Didn't he announce it?"

"No," I said. "I've been waiting right here, no more than ten feet away!"

"That couple that came in a few minutes ago—that was our hotel manager. He and his wife are leaving this morning for a vacation in Cancún. The shuttle driver left to take them to the airport."

"But how was I supposed to know who they were and where they were headed?"

"Are you sure the driver didn't announce he was going to the airport?"

"I'm sure."

"Sorry."

"OK. So what are my options for getting to the airport for a flight that leaves in forty-five minutes? I don't see any taxis out there."

"Right. We're too far out—a taxi couldn't get here in time. And they don't like to come out here anyway because we're so close to the airport. Not a big fare."

"So what are my other options?"

The desk clerk's brow furrowed.

"How far is it?" I asked.

"Not more than a mile or two. You could almost walk if you didn't have luggage and didn't have to cross three major freeways."

"Is the shuttle driver coming right back after he drops the manager off?"

"No. He was going to run some errands."

I persisted. "So how can I get to the airport?"

He thought about it, then shrugged.

"Is there *anyone* here with a car who could drive me?"

"We can't do that. Something about insurance."

"Is the manager here?"

"He just left for vacation; I told you."

"Is there an assistant manager or someone in charge while he's gone?"

"Yeah. I'll get him."

The assistant manager whistled his way out to where I stood. "What can I do for you?"

I repeated the whole story. He said, "Well, the manager was in a hurry, I guess, and didn't want to wait for anybody else."

I repeated, "My flight leaves in thirty minutes. The airport's only two miles away. How can I get there? Is there *anyone* with a car whom I can pay to drive me?"

"Let me see what I can do," he sighed, then disappeared into his office. After a moment, he reappeared in the center of the lobby with a security guard in tow. "This is John. He's going to drive you to the airport. I'd do it myself, but I really need to hang around here. Have a nice trip."

I climbed into John's pickup and caught my flight.

The extremes in the hotel managers' attitudes illustrate the essence of personal connection—and its absence.

Kim Callaway, manager of Guaranty Federal Bank's College Station banking center, received this letter from the parents of one of her college-age bank customers:

> Dear Ms. Callaway:
>
> When you send your children into the world, it is with the hope and prayers that they encounter only the best in life and that they meet and befriend people who are trusting and caring. It is one of those trusting and caring encounters which I write to you about.
>
> Earlier this month, my son Greg entered your branch to open his checking account. Several days later he said to me, "Those people were really nice! They asked me how I like A&M, and whether I was finding everything OK. Dad, they even asked me if I was having any problems!" Greg then explained to your representative that the only problem he was having was receiving mail from the family and friends. Since Greg's

telling of this story, I can assure you we have increased the mail flow between San Antonio and College Station.

However, it was not mail from Greg's family or friends that reached him first. It was the caring note from your representative: a short note that thanked Greg for opening his account with Guaranty Federal Bank and "to make sure that he had mail" in his mailbox at A&M. While this act was small and a good business practice, it was an act that meant a great deal to Greg and us, his parents.

Ms. Callaway, we do not know the name of the representative that welcomed Greg that day and followed up with the note, but please express our sincere appreciation to the caring representative and your whole staff for those caring and trusting acts.

It is so refreshing to see a bank these days doing business the right way—so refreshing that my wife and I will be investigating moving our banking business to the local Guaranty Federal Bank in our hometown.

This act of kindness is one of the many answers to our hopes and prayers. On behalf of Greg (your new customer) and his parents (future customers), thank you for caring!

A very small act with a very big payoff. How do you see the strangers who pass you every day in the workplace? Are they an interruption to your day—or the purpose of your day?

■ ■ ■

Each person's life is lived as a series of conversations.
—Dr. Deborah Tannen

We can do no great things—only small things with great love.
—Mother Teresa

How Long Will It Take?

The waiter bent down and peered under our table, and then inter-
rupted my conversation with a friend. "Excuse me. I'm so sorry."
Looking rather sheepish, he lifted my gray leather purse to eye level.
"I just spilled salad dressing on your bag."

He handed me the purse so I could inspect it myself. The lower
two inches of one side was about two shades darker than the rest. As
I examined the bag, I also noticed a green dot from a felt marker, a
remnant, no doubt, of a meeting months—or years—earlier.

He apologized and called the manager from the back to make
good.

"Can you get it cleaned for me?" I asked the manager.

"No, we can't do anything from here. But we'll be happy to reim-
burse you if you have it cleaned."

I sighed. In the space of a careless minute, another item had been
added to my to-do list in a week that was already too busy. My new
mission: Get the purse usable again before leaving town for an
upcoming convention.

Happy to be off the hook, the manager wrote me a note, promising reimbursement, and we finished our meal.

The next Saturday I began the arduous task of finding a dry cleaner
to handle the chore. All the establishments I called cleaned leather—
but not leather purses. Finally I gave up on the phone routine and
decided to try my luck as a walk-in. I figured that if they could just
see how simply the purse was designed, they'd decide it wasn't such a
different animal after all and offer to try.

The walk-in gambit didn't work much better. The Town and
Country Cleaners sent me to the Village Cleaners, who sent me to the

MidCity Cleaners, who sent me to the Quick-Stop Cleaners. Finally, I walked into a dry cleaner with a shoe-repair shop under the same roof. The clerk on duty assured me without reservation, "Yes, we clean leather purses."

Thrilled, I pushed the bag toward her and watched her write the claim ticket.

"When can I pick it up?"

"It'll take awhile. We send them out. The truck picks up only on Wednesdays. So they'll pick it up next Wednesday and then deliver it the following Wednesday. Is that OK?"

Out of habit, I opened my mouth to protest. Eleven days for cleaning?

The attendant glared at me and then shrugged in take-it-or-leave-it fashion.

I nodded acceptance, and she pushed the claim ticket toward me to fill in my name and address.

At the next counter, a guy dashed in and shoved a stack of shirts toward the clerk. He asked, "How long will these take?"

"Will tomorrow be soon enough?"

"I guess it'll have to do."

Tell me, how could he wear all those shirts the next day anyway? But me? Well, I *needed* the bag.

As the clerk finished writing her description of the purse, the thought struck me that we Americans have a penchant for asking, "How long will it take?" What we do with that information is anybody's guess. But all too often, the situation we find ourselves in is habitual hurry.

A party of eight had just placed an order for dinner in a fine restaurant: "How long will it take?" they asked. The response: "Just a few minutes, sir." Consider this: Were they going to leave if the waitress had answered, "Half an hour"? If so, why didn't they ask before they sat down and ordered?

After posing for x-rays, a patient with six fractured ribs and a broken leg asked the technician, "How long will those take?" Was he planning to play a round of golf while he waited?

I was standing in an auto-repair shop waiting for a mechanic to drive my daughter's car around after it had undergone repairs for hail damage. A woman watching a wrecker pull her smashed Toyota into the bay asked, "How long will it take?"

The mechanic chuckled, shrugged at the heap of junk that would no doubt take miracles to restore, and gave her a wry wink.

"Couple of hours, I imagine."

"Fine, thank you. Call me when it's ready," the car owner responded on her way out. Obviously she hadn't listened to or assimilated his answer. So why had she asked?

Why *do* we ask? Our lives have become clock documented and calendar driven. Our TV news broadcasts display the time on the screen. Our radio DJs announce the time every five minutes. Our computers display, track, and report each minute spent surfing the Internet, calling long-distance, and preparing Power Point presentations.

I can understand a person asking the question "How long will it take?" if he intends to pull out his dissertation and write a few paragraphs while he waits. But most of the time, the person asking the question protests, regardless of the answer. With one-hour photos, one-hour eyeglasses, and mufflers while you wait, hurry has become a cultural habit.

A friend once asked me, "Why are you rushing through life—are you in a hurry to get to the end?" He went on to list my other sins: "You talk too fast. You eat too fast. You drive too fast. You work too hard, and you're too busy to play. You're impatient." I could have added a few more vices, but I let his list suffice.

We're too impatient, too often, about too many unimportant tasks. How can God speak to us—more important, how can we listen—when we're rushing through life? How many connections with other people do we short-circuit simply because we are too busy or seem unapproachable?

Impatience prevents opportunities for connection and service. What's more, impatience often impedes solutions that might present themselves if we were more deliberate about our dealings and decisions.

Slow is a valid choice.

I told the clerk at the dry cleaner that the Wednesday after next would be fine. After all, the mark from the green felt pen has probably been there for a while. They don't even make that color anymore.

■ ■ ■

Be still, and know that I am God.

—Psalm 46:10

To know how to wait is the great secret of success.

—Joseph Marie de Maistre

Counting time is not nearly as important as making time count.

—Unknown

I must govern the clock, not be governed by it.

—Golda Meir

Tattling Pianos

Each day the tattling intensified as my two nieces played together during a string of bad weather that kept them indoors most of their spring break.

"Mommy, make Sarah put my Barbie away—she messed up the clothes."

"Mommy, make Anna come outside and clean the mud off my shoes. She splashed them, and they're all soggy."

"Mommy, make Sarah play teacher with me—she's just reading a book."

"Mommy, make Anna clean up the toothpaste in the sink. Now it's all yucky."

Finally, their mother had had enough of the tattling. She laid down the law: "I don't want to hear another tattling remark from either of you for the rest of the day. Do you hear me? Whoever comes to me to tattle is going to be in big trouble. Do you understand?"

Both girls could tell when they were walking close to the edge; they withdrew into pouting silence for a few hours. After dinner, their mother, having relaxed a bit after issuing the stern warning that had obviously worked, settled onto the couch to leaf through a magazine.

The six-year-old stood in front of her as if straining to keep something from rolling off the tip of her tongue. Her mother pretended not to notice the six-year-old's indecision. She continued to read, enjoying the evening's hard-won peace and quiet.

After a moment, six-year-old Anna eased herself onto the couch and snuggled up to her mom. When her mother absent-mindedly stretched out her arm and drew her closer for a hug, Anna could stand it no longer.

She whispered ever so sweetly, "Mommy, if you'll listen *very* carefully, you *won't* hear the sound of *any* piano playing."

I chuckled when my sister later told me about Anna's clever way of reporting that her sister had failed to practice the piano for the prescribed half-hour. I identify with that urge to report things that others might consider none of my business.

When I purchase an item that falls apart before I get it out of the package, I get the urge to report the shoddy product and its manufacturer to the Better Business Bureau. When I see a mother spending money on booze and cigarettes while yelling at her child, who is dressed in dirty rags and has a runny nose, I want to report her to a social worker for a course on parenting. When I see a teenager sitting sadly alone in church, isolated and mocked by the "in crowd" because she's different, I want to make her prom queen for a day. When I hear of the wealth of an entrepreneur who traffics in sex businesses, I want to call in the police, no matter how many city licenses the owner may have to operate.

We are shocked and then saddened by the growing violence and abuse around us: school shootings, bomb threats in public buildings, the abuse of children, pornography on the Internet, starvation of the elderly in centers that are meant to care for them.

Yes, I can definitely connect with Anna's urge to report things to the authorities. Fortunately, God is the ultimate authority, and he doesn't need our reports. We have His guarantee that one day, in His own time, He will right the wrongs and correct the injustices all around us. Evil lasts but for a season.

■ ■ ■

But men never violate the laws of God without suffering the consequences, sooner or later.

—LYDIA M. CHILD

Many seek an audience with a ruler, but it is from the LORD that man gets justice.

—PROVERBS 29:26

When Age No Longer Matters

Parked in front of a strip mall, waiting for the pharmacy to open, I sat in the car with my four-year-old in the backseat. An old friend recognized me and walked over to the passenger side of the car to chat. After a few moments, she leaned her head into the backseat window and spoke to my daughter. "And, Lisa, how are *you* this morning?"

Somewhat surprised at the personal attention from a stranger, my four-year-old turned to me and said, "She thinks I'm real."

Lisa's delighted smile struck me as peculiar. What had made her think she was invisible to older people?

In our society people tend to sort themselves by age—up to a point. The school system starts the process by herding us into grades. The nine-year-olds take math together, eat lunch together, and play soccer together. While school starts the sorting process, our kids fine-tune it. Parents cluster around the soccer field or the Barbie counter at K-Mart, not according to their own ages but according to their *kids'* ages. Parents of eight-year-olds know parents of other eight-year-olds because their *kids* take them to the same places.

But about the time our kids become teenagers, the sorting process stops. Once we're no longer forced to group ourselves by soccer matches, piano recitals, and diplomas, age becomes a less dominant factor in our selection of friends.

In college, I worked as a part-time salesclerk in a department store, along with a woman about thirty years my senior. One day she began to receive odd phone calls at work, during which she would duck her head, lower her voice, and turn away so that we could not overhear her conversation. The calls most definitely weren't from a customer asking the price of socks. One particularly busy Saturday morning, she hung up the phone in tears, so distraught that she had to leave the department for an unscheduled break. Later that day, after all the customers had gone, she confided in me. Her husband's latest lover kept calling to taunt her, threaten her, and cajole her into giving him a divorce.

Although thirty years younger than she, I understood her pain. I understood because I had known embarrassment, I had felt betrayed, I had experienced self-doubt. We connected that day on a different level—as human beings, not as middle-aged adult and teenager.

Our lives are full of such meldings of the soul, whether in joy or in pain. Eight-year-old latchkey kids befriend eighty-year-old widowers. Fifteen-year-old teens seek dating advice from forty-two-year-old coaches. Twenty-two-year-old priests share their lives with seventy-five-year-old prisoners. Movies are made of such stories.

What is it that must melt away before we stop thinking in terms of age and start thinking in terms of spirit? Does it have to involve the sharing of a tragedy such as the massacre at Columbine High School, the death of John F. Kennedy Jr., or the shooting of stockbrokers in Atlanta? Does it have to involve a person we mutually love, weaving our lives together? Does it have to involve a shared activity—bowling, boating, or Beethoven? The glue that cements us may be common values, commitments, or causes. Pain, problems, or our past.

No matter how much we tend to overlook older or younger people, they're real. Love, pain, embarrassment, jealousy, fear—the only difference in those feelings in a fourteen-year-old and a fifty-year-old is that the latter has a larger store of memories for comparison.

Maybe part of the answer to loneliness in our disconnected world is to stop using age as a determiner of friendship, Christian love, and service.

■ ■ ■

You are no longer foreigners and aliens, but fellow citizens with God's people and members of God's household.

—Ephesians 2:19

Age does not depend upon years, but upon temperament and health. Some men are born old, some never grow so.

—TRYON EDWARD

It seems as if I've been doing the same things since I was six years old. I'm a few inches taller and I have a graying beard, but otherwise there's not much difference.

—MAURICE SENDAK

Finding the Significant Season

There is a time for everything,
and a season for every activity under heaven:

a time to be born and a time to die,
a time to plant and a time to uproot,
a time to kill and a time to heal,
a time to tear down and a time to build,
a time to weep and a time to laugh,
a time to mourn and a time to dance,
a time to scatter stones and a time to gather them,
a time to embrace and a time to refrain,
a time to search and a time to give up,
a time to keep and a time to throw away,
a time to tear and a time to mend,
a time to be silent and a time to speak,
a time to love and a time to hate,
a time for war and a time for peace.
—Ecclesiastes 3:1–8

People tend to interpret this Scripture in one of two ways. The first goes something like this: "There's a time and place for what I want to do. I must go out and find it."

In this frame of mind, we shore up our courage to search for new successes—in our relationships, in our careers, in our pastimes. We reach deep within ourselves and summon the mental, physical, and emotional wherewithal to propel us out the door—to seize opportunities when they present themselves. After all, our chance may not come again. We feel an urgency to act.

If good things don't happen immediately, maybe we're just knocking on the door of opportunity too soon. If we simply bide our time, our season will come; things will fall into place for us at the right time.

When we feel as though we've beaten against a particular door of opportunity too hard and long, the idea occurs to us that maybe we should knock elsewhere. Maybe we need to go to life's next adventure without moping about "what could have been."

The second way of interpreting this passage is a fatalistic one. Some read Ecclesiastes and abandon hope, effort, and ambition.

"We're caught in a big cosmic cobweb," they say, "and everything's out of our control. Like puppets on a string, we wait for somebody either to cut the string or to set us in motion. We must dance to someone else's tune. *Qué será, será.* What will be, will be."

The choice between the two viewpoints turns on our individual attitudes toward the patterns that have been set in place in the universe.

We can live in both seasons—those with opportunities and those with limitations. Contentment comes from learning to gather in the sunshine and learning not to pout when it rains. If you expect to laugh, you must also expect to cry. Otherwise, how will you know the difference? If you're never unhappy and dissatisfied, how will you know when you're happy and satisfied?

Contentment comes from comparisons.

It's our choice. We can wake up each morning and say, "There's a purpose, a plan, and a pattern for my life. I'm safe to go out and plan and work and love until that pattern stops." Or we can wake up each morning and say, "There's a purpose, a plan, and a pattern for the universe. I'm powerless to do anything . . . to change anything . . . to be anything. What's the use?"

One viewpoint is empowering; the other, fatalistic. As Anaïs Nin observed, "We don't see things as they are, we see them as we are." Our faith dictates whether we find comfort or despair in the seasons of life. We can choose to feel safe in God's loving power and control.

Our understanding of the seasons of life also affects our relationships with others. Either we can rest in the assurance that relationships will deepen as we grow individually, or we can despair that a relationship remains on the surface much too long.

Relationships come and go, or they may deepen then stall through a lifetime of seasons. Our relationships with siblings change as we move away from our parents and into our own homes. Our relationships with coworkers sway from casual to committed and back again as projects and crises change. Our relationships with friends deepen or dim depending on whether our activities bring us into contact once a day or once a year. Dating relationships either deepen into love strong enough to support a marriage or drift into disenchantment and apathy.

Have you ever noticed that in many relationships, the harder one person tries to hold on, the further the other person pulls away? A relationship ripens only when it's not forced.

We plant the seeds of caring. We water generously. We wait, watch, weed. Wisdom is understanding that the season of dormancy precedes growth and vitality. Relationships ebb and flow in their own way in their own seasons.

■ ■ ■

My current view of the world is that life is braided streams of light and darkness, joy and pain, and I just accept them. They both exist and I walk with both, but now I know there is a choice about what I do with them.

—ARISIKA RAZAK

I discovered I always have choices and sometimes it's only a choice of attitude.

—JUDITH M. KNOWLTON

There is a time to let things happen and a time to make things happen.

—HUGH PRATHER

Turning Over a New Chapter in Life

Dramatic stories get my attention. I used to listen to guest speakers tell about their experiences with drugs, abuse, and other tragedies and wish I had a similarly persuasive story that would help others reach God for the first time or deepen their spiritual walks.

But not anymore. Not since I met Calvin.

I don't know much about Calvin's childhood; I met him when we became neighbors. That is, I met his wife and children. He was in jail. For five months he'd been locked up on various charges related to his alcoholism: drunken driving, hot checks, assault and battery. According to his wife, Lynne, he was a smart man who had let alcohol take over his life. Fighting that demon, he had lost his business, their savings, and almost his family.

One day he reappeared without warning. Lynne and I had been out for a twilight walk with our toddlers when we stopped outside her house for a drink of water. She went inside, then, looking pale and shaken, reappeared at the back door with a pitcher of ice water and glasses. "Calvin's home. He's been here to change clothes—he left his things on the chair."

His jail sentence over, he began to look for a job and make an effort to put his life back together. There were fits and false starts. Some days he looked for work; some days he drank. Some days he cursed God; some days he pleaded for forgiveness and a fresh start.

Having found a job to provide the bare necessities for their family, Lynne clung to her earlier faith in God. That relationship gave her stability in the midst of the chaos and uncertainty swirling around her. She asked close friends and the church family to pray for Calvin's salvation and his physical well-being.

There was a crusade of sorts to save Calvin's physical and spiritual life. Every time a new evangelist came to town, someone made a special effort either to get Calvin to the church service or to get the celebrity speaker to seek Calvin out for the purpose of sharing his testimony. Professional singers, polished preachers, converted movie stars, professional athletes, and powerful politicians all stopped in to talk with Calvin about the need for God in his life.

With no results. It wasn't that Calvin was rude to them; he simply remained unmoved.

During the next year, with a new job as chef at an upscale restaurant, he could once again provide for his family's physical needs. But his work was interrupted by bouts of drinking and jail time for debts and drunken brawls, and he continued to be an on-again, off-again parent and spouse.

Then one day, Lynne's small church announced a new series of meetings led by a youthful, inexperienced preacher named Ken. Lynne asked Ken to stop by their home some evening to talk with Calvin.

The preacher came. Calvin listened to what he had to say. At the conclusion of their conversation, Calvin bowed his head and asked for God's forgiveness. He made an immediate change in his life, became active in the church, and began to assume a leadership role in his family. Within weeks, Calvin began bringing his friends from his old life to their own realization of their need for God.

Frankly, I was puzzled. What had made the difference? Why had he put his wife and children through years of torment? Why had he disregarded the testimonies of so many speakers and celebrities who'd gone through similar experiences with drink or drugs? Why had he not listened to the changed Chuck Colsons of the world? Although I was thrilled at the outcome, the situation still puzzled me.

Months later as I came to know Calvin better, I posed the question to him: "How did this guy Ken get through to you when no one else could?"

"All those other people just didn't have any credibility with me," he explained.

"What do you mean? We thought you'd listen to them precisely because they'd have credibility. We thought you'd identify with all they'd been through—the drug scene, alcohol, and jail. We thought you'd speak the same language."

"We did." Calvin seemed amused.

I pressed him. "But I don't get it. This preacher Ken grew up in a regular family, became a Christian when he was nine years old, and has lived a good life ever since. What's to tell?"

Calvin again smiled at me. "I never listened to all those other people because I just figured they were turning over a new leaf. Alcoholics and prisoners do that virtually every morning of their lives. But Ken told me about a God powerful enough to keep a person away from all that junk for an entire lifetime. That got my attention."

Ever since that conversation twenty-five years ago, I've tried not to focus on dramatic, sudden changes as proof of God's power (although they are that), but on the silent strength of His hand at work in the lives of everyday people. The once unfaithful wife who now loves her husband. The once abusive manager who now respects his staff. The once bitter mother who now loves her children. The once rebellious teen who graduates with honors. The once despairing grandmother who now serves her community with hope.

Hearts can be heavy, hard, and proud. But *all* changed lives demonstrate God's power.

■ ■ ■

God does not ask your ability or your inability. He asks only your availability.

—MARY KAY ASH

He who desires to see the living God face to face should not seek him in the empty firmament of his mind, but in human love.

—FYODOR DOSTOEVSKY

A Christian is one who makes it easier for other people to believe in God.

—UNKNOWN

Everything's the
Same but Different

We called to wish Aunt Juanita a happy eighty-fourth birthday last week. To the routine question about whether she felt any older, she responded, "Actually I still feel like a teenager inside. Only my body has changed. Me—I'm the same as I ever was." Mickey Spillane agreed: "I don't feel old. I feel like a guy that something happened to."

I'm just beginning to understand that concept of aging. For the most part, society smiles playfully at the phenomenon. You may have heard some of these quips:

"Youth is a disease; age is recovering from it."

"It is possible that a man could live twice as long if he didn't spend the first half of his life acquiring habits that shorten the other half."

"You're getting over the hill when most of your dreams are reruns."

"Obsolescence too quickly follows adolescence."

(Jack Kraus)

"Old age: when actions creak louder than words."

(Dana Robbins)

"By the time a man gets to greener pastures he can't climb the fence."

(Frank Dickson)

"The seven ages of man: spills, drills, thrills, bills,
ills, pills, wills."

(Richard J. Needham)

But to some, aging is a serious issue.

Young and old alike are connected by this truth: We're the same selves we've always been; we're just camping out at different points on the aging continuum. Unless—and that's a big unless—we've made a decision to be otherwise. Let me explain.

Some simple pleasures don't change much over the years. The pleasure of talking to an old friend. Reading a good book. Feeling the cool breeze against my face during a brisk walk. Being missed when I'm away and hugged when I get home. Laughing at a stand-up comedian. Eating rocky-road ice cream in a waffle cone. Cooking a meal for company and hosting a party. Thrilling to my husband's touch.

Nor do the negatives fade away with time. Feeling tired enough to sleep twelve hours straight. Being embarrassed throughout a bad hair day. Feeling like a failure and a fraud when I don't perform to my expectations. Worrying that my kids won't drive safely. Hating to iron denim.

Yes, many of our pleasures and bothers remain with us and help define us throughout our lives, and we're all connected by this constancy. Yet in the more important aspects of life, it's how we move through the aging process itself that determines whether we grow wiser or only older.

Aging gives us perspective. Perspective means seeing the big picture and having the long view. With perspective, we know where we've been and where we're going in life. We have direction for our purpose, values from the past, awareness about the present, and peace about the future. We look at life through a broader lens as we move along.

At sixteen, a pimpled chin could send me into a dither for days. At fifty, I can hardly see it. At sixteen, an angry boyfriend could distract me from writing an English essay on a subject I knew as well as my own address. At fifty, a disgruntled husband means I don't have to cook dinner. At sixteen, a missed basket from the foul line meant that I might lose my place on the starting team. At fifty, an anecdote that bombs in a speech means that I should drop it. At sixteen, a teacher who didn't like my work made me cry and wring my hands. At fifty, an agent who doesn't like my manuscript means I need to find a new agent.

Aging and perspective give us control. When we're young, we have little control over our lives. Parents tell us what to do. Teachers tell us what to do. Neighbors tell us what to do. Friends tell us what to do. Granted, at fifty we don't have control over everything, but we certainly have options. We can decide what jobs to take, what skills to develop, and how much work we're willing to do for the life style we want. Sure, control is relative. The biggies can still throw a kink in our plans: a tornado, a merger, a heart attack. But by and large, the older we get, the more control we have over what happens to us.

Aging and perspective connect us to more people in tighter relationships. Good relationships, like good cheeses, develop through aging. The longer we know people, the smarter they become. Or maybe I should say it like this: The longer we know people, the smarter we become about their thinking, intentions, values, and strengths. We learn to appreciate others more fully for all their complexities and strengths. We judge less harshly. In essence, our essence becomes synchronized with their essence. The roots grow deeper. They offer stronger support. We allow ourselves to drink from their wells.

Perspective—and Aunt Juanita—tells me that the real me will be the same no matter how gravity works. We all grow old. It's up to each of us individually to grow better and deeper.

■ ■ ■

Life is change. Growth is optional. Choose wisely.

—Karen Kaiser Clark

Preparation for old age should begin not later than one's teens. A life which is empty of purpose until sixty-five will not suddenly become filled on retirement.

—Arthur Morgan

Some lives, like evening primroses, blossom most beautifully in the evening of life.

—Charles E. Cowman

How many fancy they have experience simply because they have grown old.

—Stanislaus

Creative Bones in Your Body

Creativity may involve only looking at something in a new way. For example, did you know that right and left shoes were thought of only a little more than a century ago?

"There's not a creative bone in my body," my mother used to say. Yet the rest of her family has enjoyed her creative flair for years. Almost single-handedly, this tiny 106-pound woman has remodeled houses, removed walls, added closets, built staircases, and wall-papered and Sheetrocked bedrooms at the drop of a dime. We rarely sit down to a holiday meal without enjoying the sight of a centerpiece she has just created—from pastel Easter-egg trees to abundant cornucopias at Thanksgiving. She also happens to be a whiz with a sewing machine and can make anything from dresses to dust ruffles to drapes. Although she minimizes her talent, the rest of the family notices and appreciates her creations.

It's a universal truth: Acts of creation seem to take at least two people—the creator and the person who enjoys the creation. That connection between the two people gives both people purpose.

Ask those who create things as a hobby, and they'll tell you that praise and appreciation cause their creativity to blossom while the discouragement of detractors turns off the flow—and the joy—completely. For verification of that principle, ask baseball players who've been in a slump for months. Or novelists who've been suffering from writer's block for years. Or soloists who haven't performed in concert in a decade.

I became starkly aware of this connection about fifteen years ago while I was doing a video series for Encyclopaedia Britannica. Britannica had contracted with me to do a series of video training programs on communication skills for their corporate clients. So they flew me to their studio in Chicago to tape the series before a live audience. No problem. Members of the audience laughed at my anecdotes when they were supposed to, looked reflective when I made an important point, and answered questions as I tossed them out—all the responses you'd expect from a live audience.

When my producer sent me the raw footage of the sessions for review, I marked several places where I'd flubbed my words. I then flew back to Chicago for a day of retakes. But this time, there was no live audience—just a camera and the producer and me in a room. Yes, I thought I was energetic and demonstrative the second time around. But when both recording sessions were spliced together and I saw the edited version, I was appalled. As I watched the tape, I could pinpoint every single inserted sentence or section. The difference in my energy was dramatic.

The producer explained that that's always the case—it's the difference between connecting with an audience and, well, the dynamics of entertaining four blank walls.

To be our most creative selves at home and at work, we need others who appreciate and enjoy our work. Their response is our vitamin. Look for them. Connect with them. Create for them.

Yet sometimes it's not a lack of appreciation but the shallowness of the well inside that limits our creativity. According to Goethe, "If you would *create* something, you must *be* something." And as the old Chinese proverb says, "Be not afraid of growing slowly; be afraid only of standing still." As creators, we have to refill our water jugs often. My friend, Charlie "Tremendous" Jones sums it up this way: "You're the same today as you'll be in five years—except for the people you meet and the books you read."

To create output, we have to take in spiritual nourishment. We have to become.

Albert Einstein gave us another clue about creativity: "In my experience, the best creative work is never done when one is unhappy." When you think about it, creation is a lonely act. Maybe even a struggle. In reality, creativity involves reaching inside yourself and pulling an idea or performance from your soul. Doing something creative involves putting yourself—your ideas, your soul, your mind, your effort—"out there" for the whole world to see. That willingness involves risk and courage. If Einstein was correct, then creators need to connect. Contentment, for most, comes from connection with others.

So, for creators to perform at their best, they must know that their acts of creation have been accepted and appreciated by others. They must have something inside to give. And to reach their full creative potential, they must be contented.

Finally, creators need to deliver the goods. The compulsion to deliver our creativity to someone else is evidenced by the quest of new writers to become published authors. It is not enough to write poems and stories and stack them in a drawer. Creative people take the risk of putting their creations "out there" for others to enjoy or reject—that's part of the process for them. In fact, many people have spent their lives and great sums of their own money publishing their own books in an effort to connect their creative efforts to an appreciative audience.

You see this urge at work every day at home and at the office. Gardeners create for those who appreciate the beauty of flowers. Cooks create for those who appreciate their gourmet meals. Painters create for those who love color and design. Singers create for those who are moved by their songs. Playwrights create for those who want to build their lives around new insights. Comedians create for those who love to laugh. Preachers create for those who want inspiration to achieve their full potential. Mothers create character in their children for the good of the children and society itself.

Although many people create in private, their connection to others proves essential to continued creativity. That human connection often proves strong enough to overcome obstacles to creativity such as poverty, fatigue, too little time, frustration, loneliness, and the status quo.

When Alexander the Great visited Diogenes and asked whether he could do anything for the famed teacher, Diogenes replied, "Only stand out of my light." We know so little about how to heighten creativity. But until we learn those secrets, maybe one of the best things we can do for the creative men and women in our lives is to stand out of their light. And appreciate their work.

God is the author of creativity. As Mary Daly observed, "It is the creative potential itself in human beings that is the image of God." And when we appreciate the creativity of others—and tell them so— we empower each other to use our talents as God designed.

■ ■ ■

Creativity is not dulled by age, only by disuse.
—O. ALDRICH WAKEFORD

Creativity is more than just being different. Anybody can play weird; that's easy. What's hard is to be simple as Bach. Making the simple complicated is commonplace; making the complicated simple, awesomely simple, that's creativity.
—CHARLES MINGUS

Creation is a better means of self-expression than possession; it is through creating, not possessing, that life is revealed.
—VIDA D. SCUDDER

You'll Have to Go Ask Him

Sometimes, when traveling hiccups get started, they just won't stop. That was the case during my stay at a five-star hotel in the West Palm Beach, Florida, area not long ago. When I checked in at the front desk, I asked for my messages or faxes. The clerk said there were none.

But when I walked into my room, the message light on the phone was blinking. I called the front desk to learn that I did, in fact, have a fax waiting. "Sorry. I caught my mistake just after you walked away from the desk. So I've already asked the bellman to bring it to your room. He should be there any moment."

I thanked her and hung up.

Thirty minutes passed. No bellman.

I phoned the bell captain's stand. "Well, I just came on duty. I don't know anything about a fax." I gave him the details.

I unpacked, took a bath, and watched the news on TV. Two hours later, still no fax. I phoned the bell captain's stand again. The supervisor answered, "Sorry, but we can't find the fax. The front desk shouldn't have told you we had it, because we don't. We don't know anything about it. You'll need to call the front desk again."

I phoned the front desk. Again. "Sorry. I gave the fax to the bellman, Mike, but he has gone home now. I'll try to catch him at home. And as soon as we reach him and find out where he put the fax, we'll get it to you."

I gave up on the fax and went to bed.

The next morning when I checked out of the hotel, it was raining. I handed the parking valet my ticket for the rental car, then watched him scurry from one side of the parking lot to the other in his yellow slicker. Five minutes, then ten minutes passed. Finally he came back inside. "I can't find your car."

"Don't you have the number of the parking spot on the claim ticket?"

"Yes," he nodded, "but the car's not there. It's not where it's supposed to be. The night people never do things right. When they park cars in the overflow lot, they never think to tell us on the morning crew." He added, "I guess I could go try again. Would you describe it to me?"

I decided to try to locate the car myself because I couldn't afford to wait another ten minutes. As I put up my umbrella and headed outside, he called after me, "I'm sorry. I just wish other people would do things right. I don't know how to find a car that somebody else lost."

That's not the end of my experience at that hotel. On the flight home, I remembered leaving my bathrobe hanging on the back of the bathroom door. So three hours later, when I arrived home, I phoned the hotel and spoke to the agent at the front desk.

"I accidentally left my robe hanging on the bathroom door in Room 225. Would you please have it mailed to me?"

"I'll connect you with housekeeping. They handle that," she said, clicking off the line without waiting for a response.

I repeated the situation to the housekeeping supervisor. She said, "I don't have time to go look for a robe. I've got to get my girls out on the floors. You'll have to call back later when I have more time." She hung up.

I called back an hour later and asked for housekeeping. The supervisor had the robe.

"Great. Thanks for checking. Would you please mail it to me?"

"I don't have authority to do that because the night crew found it. You'll have to talk to somebody on the night crew."

"Could you switch me back to the front desk then?"

"Can't. I don't know how this phone system works. I just get incoming calls."

I hung up, dialed the hotel again, and asked to speak to the manager. I reported the details of the ongoing robe saga.

The manager said, "I'm appalled that housekeeping would tell you they can't mail a package or transfer a call. That's ridiculous. I'll personally go get the robe and see that it's mailed to you. What's your address?"

I gave her the address and my Federal Express number.

A week later the robe still had not arrived.

I phoned the manager again. "Do you mean you still haven't gotten that robe? I went down there and got it myself. Let me check into it and see what happened. People are so undependable."

She was telling me?

Another week passed. Still no robe.

I made a third phone call to the manager. She said, rather indignantly, "Would you give me the address again? I'll see what I can do to get it mailed out today."

As I thought about the frustration and time involved in my experience with this hotel, it occurred to me what a mess we'd be in if God gave us the same runaround when we asked for his help or answer to a problem.

To date in my communion with him, I don't recall ever hearing any of these responses: "You'll have to call someone else." Or "That's not my area." Or "I don't know how to handle this." Customer-service reps don't always follow through. Coworkers disappoint us. Even family members let us down from time to time. But my heart feels lighter when I consider that God is always available, always concerned, always in control, always competent, always powerful enough to meet my needs. The least of which is a bathrobe.

■ ■ ■

My grandfather once told me that there are two kinds of people: those who do the work and those who take the credit. He told me to try to be in the first group; there is much less competition.

—INDIRA GANDHI

God's main problem with the laborers in his vineyard is absenteeism.

—UNKNOWN

It should be a great comfort to know that God still has his hands on the steering wheel of the universe.

—UNKNOWN

Jesus Christ is the same yesterday and today and forever.

—HEBREWS 13:8

Gratitude to God should be as regular as our heartbeat.

—UNKNOWN

Birthdays That Count . . . and Count . . . and Count

At two, birthdays don't make a lot of sense to you. But you're excited about the excitement. There's a party at your house to which your older brothers and sisters, grandparents, aunts, uncles, and cousins are invited. They hang balloons and paint clowns on the cake. They ruffle your hair, toss you in the air, and coax you to pucker up and blow hot air toward the candles. You don't yet understand price tags, so you love the cardboard boxes as much as the cars and trucks inside them. All the attention makes you scamper, scream, and sparkle.

At ten, birthdays can make or break your social standing. You have a party at a place other than home, such as a bowling alley, skating rink, or McDonald's. You definitely don't invite your grandparents, aunts, uncles, or siblings. You need at least ten other ten-year-olds to make it worthwhile. Instead of the balloons, they give you and your friends a stack of quarters for the vid-kid games, and you're on your own for entertainment. Your parents do a better job with gifts because you've given them a list from which to select and you've noted the preferred brand names.

At eighteen, birthdays cause friction. Your folks know that shopping will be a problem and worry that they won't buy the right gift. They're right to worry—the gift is always wrong. If they buy jeans, they won't fit. If they buy jewelry, it'll be the wrong color. No parties. You'd rather do your own thing. So twenty-nine of your closest friends go out for pizza and hang out together. That's the real party. Then your folks either cook a nice dinner or take you out to eat and pretend that theirs is the real party. You promise yourself that when you have kids of your own, you'll find out what they really want and do their birthdays up right.

At thirty, birthdays are inconvenient. *What's wrong with me?* you ask yourself midafternoon. *It's my* birthday—*so am I going to work on my birthday, too? Am I becoming an unbalanced social outcast, or what?* You don't like the answers you're coming up with, so you decide to leave early and *do* something. After all, what are you working so hard for if you can't enjoy yourself on your birthday? Your spouse phones before you leave. "It's your birthday, hon, so what do you want to do?"

"I don't know." You're a little disappointed that your spouse hasn't already made plans, hired a sitter, and arranged for a limo.

"Well, let's do *something*. Don't worry about this project I'm working on. It can wait. If I get fired, I get fired."

"So you really need to work, huh?"

"No, it's OK. It's your *birthday*."

You hustle the kids to a sitter. Your relatives call as you're dressing. The dishwasher backs up and empties onto the floor. At dinner, you eat a sinful dessert because you earn good money and deserve it. The next Saturday, you and your spouse buy a dishwasher for your birthday present.

At fifty, birthdays are a note on the office calendar. You hope your colleagues won't embarrass you with some kind of cake and a clown in a tutu. They do; you smile graciously, hoping no one will ask your real age. For after-dinner entertainment at home, you and your spouse read the newspaper together. Both kids call before bedtime and ask if you got the card. They want a big thank-you for having remembered. And by the way, the card took their last dime.

Thank goodness, it's over and nobody commented on the weight gain or the hairline.

At seventy-five, birthdays become important again. You wonder who will remember and make a fuss. That's the part that you never know until the phone or doorbell rings. You've totally forgotten about gifts until someone shows up with one. Heaven knows, the family needs a reason to get together and if your birthday marks the event, so be it. They all show up—and that's the best part. You decide that birthdays should get more attention; families need them to reflect and repair strained relationships.

At ninety, birthdays become a cause for community celebration. Not many people actually know who you are or what you've done, but they show up just to pay their respects to someone who's either beaten the odds or been very blessed. Anybody might decide to give you a party. You've outlived your parents, siblings, and most of your friends, so the event is hosted by neighbors, children, or grandchildren (all great). Your name is mentioned on the radio, in the church bulletin, and in the newspaper. Somebody brings a video camera. People whose names you don't recognize send cards. There aren't many gifts, however, because most people can't figure out what you can still see, hear, or eat. They act as though you've lost your mind, saying silly things about how young you look and betting you can still outwork, outdance, outplay, or outsing them any day.

Total strangers feel compelled to speak to you and give you things—a handmade card from their kindergartner, a rose from their patio, a snapshot of a tree. At some point, the occasion becomes solemn, religious. It causes people to consider their own mortality.

Most birthdays come and go. But a few stay with you. What makes birthdays meaningful? Your connection with people and your own peace of mind at the time. Widen your circle of friends each year. Surround yourself with two kinds of people: those you love and those who need your love.

■ ■ ■

For the ignorant, old age is a winter; for the learned, it is a harvest.

—JEWISH PROVERB

People usually feel that they reached forty prematurely. Forty is the age when you begin to realize how much fun you had when you were twenty.

—UNKNOWN

It's so sad that people are like plants—some go to seed with age and others go to pot.

—UNKNOWN

We look into mirrors, but we only see the effects of our times on us—not our effects on others.

—PEARL BAILEY

About the Author

A prolific author of more than thirty-seven books, Dianna Booher is CEO of Dallas–Fort Worth-based Booher Consultants, a training firm specializing in communication skills. Her career as a professional speaker puts her in front of audiences ranging from churches to corporations. *Successful Meetings* magazine recently named Dianna to their list of "Top Twenty-one Speakers for the Twenty-first Century." Her clients include IBM, ExxonMobil, Hewlett Packard, Lockheed Martin, Fujitsu, Frito-Lay, MCI WorldCom, Texas Instruments, Morgan Stanley Dean Witter, Salomon Smith Barney, and Deloitte & Touche, among others. She holds a master's degree from the University of Houston. She lives in the Dallas–Fort Worth metroplex with her husband, Vernon Rae.

For More Information

If you would like more information regarding scheduling a workshop or a keynote speech, please contact:

Booher Consultants, Inc.
4001 Gateway Drive
Colleyville, TX 76034-5917
Phone: 817-868-1200
E-mail: mailroom@booherconsultants.com
Web site: www.booherconsultants.com

Other Resources by Dianna Booher

Books

Mother's Gifts to Me: Lessons for Living and Loving

The Worth of a Woman's Words

The Little Book of Big Questions: Answers to Life's Perplexing Questions

Love Notes: From My Heart to Yours

Ten Smart Moves for Women Who Want to Succeed in Love and Life

Fresh-Cut Flowers for a Friend

Get a Life Without Sacrificing Your Career

Communicate with Confidence: How to Say It Right the First Time
   and Every Time

Get Ahead; Stay Ahead

The Complete Letterwriter's Almanac

Clean Up Your Act: Effective Ways to Organize Paperwork
   and Get It Out of Your Life

Cutting Paperwork in the Corporate Culture

Executive's Portfolio of Model Speeches for All Occasions

First Thing Monday Morning

Would You Put That in Writing?

Writing for Technical Professionals

Good Grief, Good Grammar

The New Secretary: How to Handle People as Well as You Handle Paper

Send Me a Memo: A Handbook of Model Memos

To the Letter: A Handbook of Model Letters for the Busy Executive

Great Personal Letters for Busy People

Winning Sales Letters

67 Presentations: Secrets to Wow Any Audience

To-the-Point E-Mail and Voice Mail

Videotapes

Basic Steps for Better Business Writing (series)

Business Writing: Quick, Clear, Concise

Closing the Gap: Gender Communication Skills

Cutting Paperwork: Management Strategies
Cutting Paperwork: Support Staff Strategies

Audiotape Series

People Power
Write to the Point: Business Communications from Memos to Meetings

Software (Disks and CD-ROMs)

Effective Writing
Effective Editing
Good Grief, Good Grammar
More Good Grief, Good Grammar
Ready, Set, NeGOtiate
2001 Letters That Work
2001 Business Letters
2001 Sales and Marketing Letters
Model Personal Letters
8005 Model Quotes, Speeches, and Toasts

Workshops

Effective Writing
Technical Writing
To-the-Point E-Mail and Voice Mail
Developing Winning Proposals
Good Grief, Good Grammar
Customer Service Communications
Increasing Your Personal Productivity
Presentations That Work (oral presentations)
People Power (interpersonal skills)
People Productivity (interpersonal skills)
Listening Until You Really Hear
Resolving Conflict Without Punching Someone Out
Leading and Participating in Productive Meetings
Negotiating So That Everyone Feels Like a Winner

Speeches

The Gender Communication Gap: "Did You Hear What I Think I Said?"

Communication: From Boardroom to Bedroom

Communication: The 10 Cs

Selling Across Gender Lines

Communicating CARE to Customers

Write This Way to Success

Platform Tips for the Presenter

Get a Life Without Sacrificing Your Career

Putting Together the Puzzle of Personal Excellence

The Plan and the Purpose—Despite the Pain and the Pace

Ten Smart Moves for Women

The Worth of a Woman's Words

Words can protect, promise, or punish; affirm, advise, or accuse.

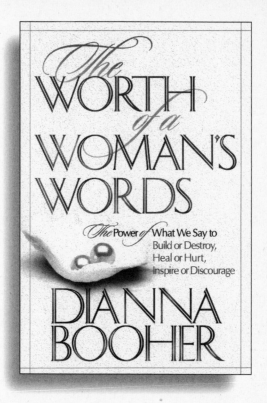

In **The Worth of a Woman's Words,** *Dianna Booher shows how words can be heard long after they are spoken.*

With heartwarming stories and thought-provoking quotes and Scriptures, Dianna Booher offers 41 ways a woman's words can build, heal, and encourage—and 29 ways words can discourage or destroy. This book will challenge you to think about the ways your words affect others, and encourage you to use them wisely, deliberately, and well.

Ⓦ WORD PUBLISHING

www.wordpublishing.com